The New York Yacht Club:
1844-1994

Charles M. Leighton
Commodore

A. L. Loomis III
Vice Commodore

Robert L. James
Rear Commodore

Foreword

Late in the afternoon on Sunday, July 30, 1844, nine sailing friends gathered in the cabin of John Stevens's yacht GIMCRACK, which was anchored off the Battery in New York Harbor. He informed them he intended to form a yacht club and that they were all members. The only other item of business was to set a date for the first annual cruise to Newport which started at 0900 three days later. In this abrupt manner, the New York Yacht Club was officially launched with a desire to race sailing yachts in a congenial atmosphere. From that historic meeting 150 years ago has grown a tradition of great yacht racing that is unparalleled in the world today. Whether they were competitively racing their own yachts or sponsoring boats like AMERICA, their quest for speed and sportsmanship were paramount. This wonderful book brings to life the New York Yacht Club sailboats and skippers who throughout time have kept this tradition alive.

As our sesquicentennial year draws to a close, the Club's enduring mission to "promote the highest form of Corinthian seamanship in national and international yachting forums and yacht racing competitions." continues. That was clearly the objective of our Sesquicentennial Regatta. Together with the Royal Thames Yacht Club, the Royal Yacht Squadron, the Royal Bermuda Yacht Club, the Royal Sydney Yacht Squadron and the Royal Perth Yacht Club (who, with the New York Yacht Club, have a combined 958 years of contribution to the world of yacht racing), we have witnessed its success. Two hundred fourteen yachts and some 2,700 sailors participated in a magnificent week of superb racing.

Each of us has our own memory of the magic of the sea. My favorite comes from a description of the New York Yacht Club Cruise in 1883 from Newport, Rhode Island, to Maine. "It's difficult to romanticize the fog when one has sailing in mind. Sailing in a thick fog does not suggest itself as an amusement...but when the fog lifts, all discomforts past and to come are forgotten for awhile in the sheer delight of the beauty of the day."

I would like to wish you all "the sheer delight of the beauty of the day."

Charles M. Leighton

Commodore Charles M. Leighton
November 1994

The New York Yacht Club:

1844-1994

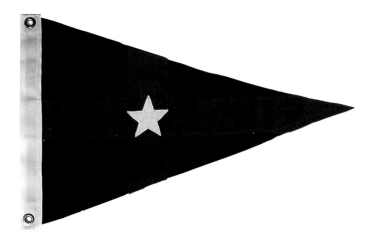

This book has been written in celebration of the 150th anniversary of the founding of the New York Yacht Club. It is dedicated to the Club's members of the past, present and future.

By Melissa H. Harrington

GREENWICH PUBLISHING GROUP, INC.
LYME, CONNECTICUT

Produced and published by Greenwich Publishing Group, Inc.,
Lyme, Connecticut

Design by Clare Cunningham Graphic Design,
Essex, Connecticut

Separation & film assembly by Silver Eagle Graphics, Inc.

This book is printed on acid-free paper.

Awful Awful® is a registered trademark of Newport Creamery, Inc.

Library of Congress Catalog Card Number: 94-72875

ISBN: 0-944641-07-5

First Printing: December 1994

Table of Contents

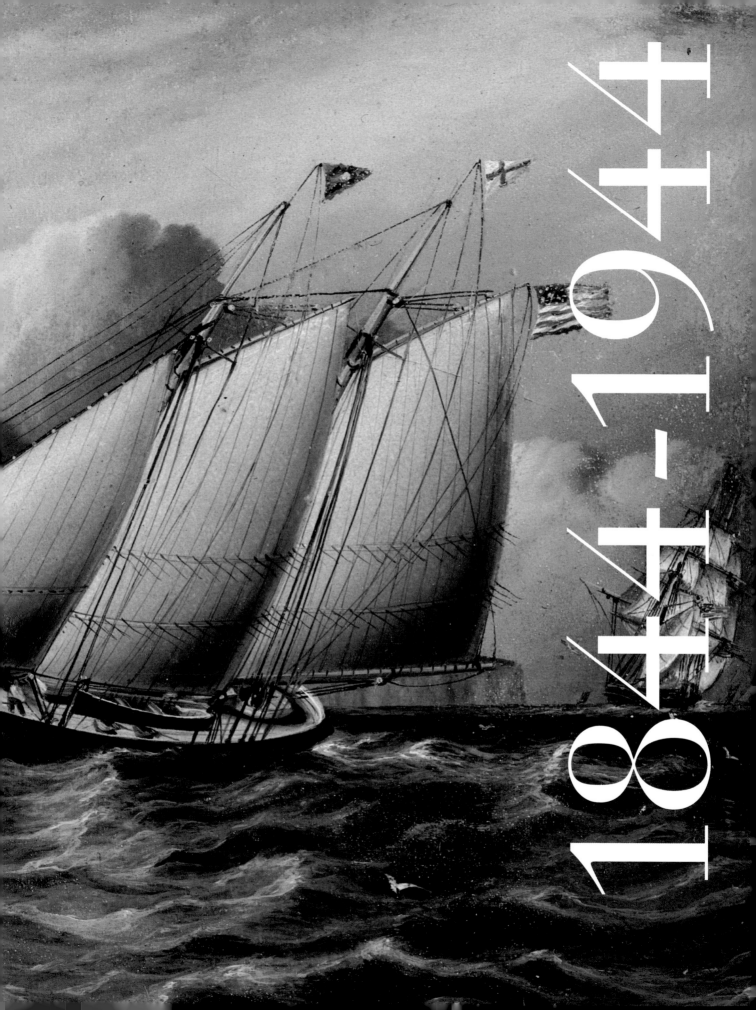

1844-1944

Sailboat racing in New York Harbor has always been an exciting event calling for spit and polish and finery all around. A newspaper description of the 1868 Regatta scene portrayed in this engraving of the New York Yacht Club clubhouse at Clifton, Staten Island, could, with a little imagination, describe the 150th Open Fall Regatta held in September 1994; "The waters of the Narrows were clogged with flag-bedecked boats of all descriptions — small sailboats, sloops, schooners, densely crowded steamers and elegant steam-driven yachts with bands aboard to supply music for the ladies."

The New York Yacht Club has been an organization of remarkable achievement for all its 150 years. Auspiciously, it was founded on a yacht, and equally auspiciously, some might say, it was born with a certain autocratic air. Our founder scarcely could have been surprised when the friends he had invited to his yacht anchored off the Battery on that July day in 1844 voted him the first Commodore or approved the only business he put before that founding meeting — that the new club's first cruise begin three days later.

It was a regional, even a national, club from its beginning. Its first clubhouse was not in New York but in New Jersey. And barely four years after its

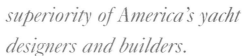

This 1880 watercolor by Frederick S. Cozzens, "Schooner in Calm Waters," is one painting of a triptych that hangs in the 44th Street Club House.

founding, its prominence was such that the United States government asked it to design a flag that would fly only on pleasure vessels. That flag, unchanged from the original New York Yacht Club design, has been the U.S. yacht ensign ever since.

And a scarce seven years after its founding, the Club's burgee flew over the yacht AMERICA as it established in that famous race off Cowes the superiority of America's yacht designers and builders.

The Club's first century and a half, as captured in this sesqui-centennial volume, is a dramatic story of winners and losers, gallant gentlemen and an occasional spoilsport, great yachts and real adventurers united by their relentless quest for speed under sail. Its proud history is, indeed, one for the book.   — Walter Cronkite

Minutes of the

New York Yacht Club

on board of the "Gimcrack" off
the Battery July 30ᵗʰ 1844, 5. P. m.

According to previous notice the
following Gentlemen assembled
for the purpose of organizing
a Yacht Club — viz

    John C. Stevens   Dead
    Hamilton Wilkes   Dead
1 William Edgar
2 John C. Jay   Out
3 George L. Schuyler
    Louis A. Depaw   Out
4 George B. Rollins
5 James M. Waterbury
6 James Rogers   Out

On Motion, it was resolved to
form a Yacht Club —
On Motion, it was resolved, that
the Title of the Club be " the.
New York Yacht Club
On Motion it was resolved that the
Gentlemen present be the original

At 1700 on Tuesday, July 30, 1844, John Cox Stevens, far right, assumed a title that was new to the world: Commodore of the New York Yacht Club. He staged the Club's founding very carefully. His yacht GIMCRACK, right, aboard which the first meeting took place, was anchored off the Battery to host the eight yachtsmen, including George L. Schuyler, above, whom he had chosen as co-founders. A little leather-bound volume, left, was on board for the purpose of recording the proceedings. The original minute book is the sole survivor of that founding meeting and resides today in a leather box kept carefully under lock and key at the Club House.

The Founding Aboard GIMCRACK-1844

Founding Commodore John Cox Stevens (1785-1857) invited eight yachting friends to a meeting aboard his 51-foot yacht GIMCRACK, anchored off the Battery in New York Harbor, at 1700 on July 30, 1844. They were Louis A. Depau, William Edgar, John C. Jay, James Rogers, George B. Rollins, George L. Schuyler, James M. Waterbury and Hamilton Wilkes, and they were invited for a very specific purpose. As recorded in the little leather-bound book kept today at the Club House, they "resolved to form a Yacht Club, that the title of the Club be the New York Yacht Club...that the gentlemen present be the original members of the Club...and that John C. Stevens be the Commodore." Further, "after appointing Friday 2nd August at 0900 the time for sailing on the Cruise, the Meeting Adjourned."

John Cox Stevens grew up in Hoboken, New Jersey, and spent his childhood sailing on the Hudson River (then referred to as the North River) with his three brothers. Soon after graduating from Columbia College in 1803, he joined his distinguished father, a Revolutionary War general, and brothers in the designing and development of steam-powered vessels. At age 24, he single-handedly built DOVER, a 20-foot sailboat. A

lifelong fascination with the engineering challenges of speed afloat under both power and sail resulted in a long line of successors to DOVER. By 1844, he owned GIMCRACK, designed by George Steers.

Yachting in New York City in the 1840s was a relatively new and extremely popular spectator sport. In addition to thronging the shores to watch sailboat races, the public — as well as the participants — particularly enjoyed wagering on the outcome of these matches. The geography of the harbor made regatta viewing accessible to all, and it made sailing the centerboard vessels of the day (which were built to handle New York Harbor's shoals), great sport for both participants and observers. In short, the climate was perfect for the creation of a yacht club, and John Cox Stevens, "the father of the sport of yachting in America," was the leading businessman and sportsman of the time who could make it come to pass. With him began the New York Yacht Club. About him came the Club saying, "once a Commodore, always a Commodore."

MR. J. C. STEVENS' "GIMCRACK."

The Clubhouse with Three Lives

Designed by Alexander Jackson Davis, the original home of the New York Yacht Club is a small Gothic building with gingerbread trim. It was built in 1845 in Elysian Fields, near Hoboken, New Jersey, just across the Hudson River from Manhattan. The site was a popular picnic area for New Yorkers and had been owned by Commodore John Cox Stevens. The first meeting in the new clubhouse took place on July 15, 1845, less than a year after the Club's founding aboard GIMCRACK.

The building served as the center of the Club's yachting activities for 23 years. By 1868, increased membership and crowded racing conditions off Hoboken caused the Club to move to Clifton, Staten Island, just north of where the Verrazano Narrows Bridge is today. The New Jersey Yacht Club took over the old building.

By 1904, the clubhouse had been given back to the Club by the Pennsylvania Railroad which had purchased the land on which it sat for a track extension. Commodore Frederick G. Bourne arranged for the building to be placed on a barge and towed to Glen Cove, Long Island, then the principal site of Club racing, where it became Station No. 10.

The final chapter of the building's history began 45 years later. At a Club meeting in April 1949, the membership decided to sell the Glen Cove property but retain the clubhouse. The primary reason for the decision to close what was to be the Club's last station was the post-World War II trend away from large racing yachts; the smaller yachts, which could easily fit into other anchorages, did not need the depth and openness of the Glen Cove harbor.

The clubhouse was again placed on a barge and towed down the Sound to Mystic Seaport where it is on "indefinite loan" to the museum. Funding for the move came from Commodore J. Burr Bartram and his family in memory of their father. An enduring eyewitness to the Club's first 150 years, the building is currently used for exhibits and is open to Seaport visitors.

The gingerbread-style original New York Yacht Club clubhouse in its three incarnations: at Elysian Fields, opposite page, above, it was the site and witness of many Club firsts; opposite page, bottom, as Station No. 10 at Glen Cove for 45 years before it was moved, right, to its current and final resting place at Mystic Seaport. The building can also be seen in the painting on the following page.

The first New York Yacht Club Regatta, billed as a "trial of speed," was sailed on the Hudson River (then referred to as the North River) off the Elysian Fields clubhouse on July 17, 1845, less than a year after the founding of the Club. Nine yachts were started with individual guns fired from the steamboat WAVE, having previously been furnished with a "memorandum of the order of getting under way." Although starting last and almost going aground on the flats, CYGNET won the 40-mile race around the Lower Harbor and back to Elysian Fields in 5 hours and 26 minutes, showing that "a good model, a good breeze and good

In 1846, the second Annual Regatta, below, lists NORTHERN LIGHT, BRENDA and COQUETTE, three large and very fast visitors from Boston. The light-air race was won by the much smaller 44-ton New York Yacht Club sloop MIST.

management were superior in this instance to steam." This painting of the first regatta by A.D. Blake was commissioned by the Club for its sesquicentennial.

ENTRIES

FOR

JULY 17, 1846.

TIME OF STARTING:

					H.	M.	S.
Schr. Gimcrack	25 tons	Stevens	10	1	30
" Hornet	25 "	Barker	10	1	30
Sloop Pearsall	27 "	Pearsall	10	3	00
Schr. Mist	30 "	Acker	10	5	15
" Brenda	32 "	Sears	10	7	30
" Mist	44 "	Depau	10	15	45
" Cygnet	45 "	Suydam	10	18	30
Sloop Ann Maria	52 "	Clark	10	21	45
" Dart	59 "	Talman	10	27	00
Schr. Siren	72 "	Miller	10	32	30
" Coquette	75 "	Perkins	10	30	45
Northern Lights	70	Winchester	10	33	15

The time is that allowed for tonnage in starting.

The Best Boat in the World

To this day, many marine artists feel the canon by which they are judged is their portrayal of the schooner AMERICA. Painted circa 1855, this unsigned primitive painting of AMERICA sailing off Cowes features disproportionately sized flags and human figures.

In the fall of 1850, a letter from a London correspondent circulated around New York City and eventually came to the attention of Commodore John C. Stevens. The letter suggested that a boat be sent to the first International Exposition at the Crystal Palace in London as an example of the excellence of American shipbuilding and design.

The project was a perfect fit for Stevens and a group of sailing colleagues, most of whom were Club members. They formed a syndicate to produce the best boat the United States of America could muster. Two bright talents were immediately enlisted for the venture: George Steers, well known to the syndicate and designer of the MARY TAYLOR, the state-of-the-art pilot boat of the time, was commissioned to design the vessel; Captain Dick Brown, owner of the MARY TAYLOR and dean of the Sandy Hook pilots, was hired to sail her. (Pilot boats were the fastest of the day, as numerous vessels vied for the business of placing a harbor pilot on board in-bound vessels. In a first-come, first-served world, speed was paramount.)

No jaunty, light name for this craft; the self-conscious mantle it assumed was a portent of things to come. AMERICA the mission, the legend, the beautiful, was launched on May 3, 1851. Following

Larger-than-life Captain Dick Brown, left, died as he lived his entire life, as a Sandy Hook pilot. In 1885, at age 75, Brown spent a freezing February night piloting a freighter into the Port of New York. By the time he left his post in the morning, his foot had frozen. Gangrene soon attacked his foot, and he died four months later.

sea trials and sporting a set of working sails borrowed from the MARY TAYLOR for its transatlantic passage, AMERICA sailed on June 21 for Le Havre, where she would be outfitted and spiffed up for the coming races. The Stevens party and other syndicate members traveled to France by steamer and met the boat at the dock when it arrived 20 days and 6 hours later.

AMERICA sailed for England on July 30, heavily loaded with provisions and extra sails which set her five inches down on her marks. John Cox Stevens tells the story of her arrival in Cowes:

> In coming from Havre, we were obliged, by the darkness of the night and a thick fog, to anchor some five or six miles from Cowes. In the morning early the tide was against us, and it was dead calm. At nine o'clock a gentle breeze sprang up, and with it came gliding down the LAVEROCK, one of the newest and fastest cutters of her class. The news spread like lightning that the Yankee clipper had arrived, and that the LAVEROCK had gone down to show her the way up.
>
> The yachts and vessels in the harbor, the wharves, and windows of all the houses bordering on them, were filled with thousands of spectators, watching, with eager eyes, the eventful trial they saw we could not escape; for the LAVEROCK stuck to us, sometimes lying to, and sometimes tacking around us, evidently showing she had no intention of quitting us.
>
> We got up our sails with heavy hearts — the wind had increased to a five or six knot breeze, and after waiting until we were ashamed to wait longer, we let her get about two hundred yards ahead, and then started in her wake. I have seen and been engaged in many exciting trials at sea and on shore, without feeling one-hundredth part of the responsibility, and without suffering one-hundredth part of the fear and dread I felt at the thought of being beaten by the LAVEROCK in this eventful trial. During the first five minutes, not a sound was heard, save, perhaps, the beating of our anxious hearts or the slight ripple of the water upon our sword-like stem.
>
> The captain was crouched upon the floor of the cockpit, his seemingly unconscious hand upon the tiller, with his stern unaltering gaze upon the vessel ahead. The men were motionless as statues, with their eager eyes fastened upon the LAVEROCK with a fixedness and intensity that seemed almost unnatural. It could not, and did not, last long. We worked quickly and surely to windward of her wake. The crisis was past, and some dozen of deep-drawn sighs proved that the agony was over.

While that early-morning sail into Cowes was never meant to be a race, a race it was — LAVEROCK was bested by the American visitor. The Britishers, led by the Earl of Wilton, commodore of the Royal Yacht Squadron, who came to greet them, knew this was a boat to be reckoned with.

John C. Stevens then issued an open challenge to race "any number of schooners belonging to any of the yacht squadrons of the kingdom, to be selected by the commodore of the Royal Yacht Squadron;" the race to be sailed in at least a six-knot breeze. But the Britishers, having seen how effortlessly AMERICA sailed against LAVEROCK, knew a serious threat when they saw one, and there were no takers.

Stevens then posted a notice in the clubhouse offering to race "any British vessel whatsoever, for any sum from 1 to 10,000 guineas," the only stipulation again being that there was at least a six-knot breeze. Still no takers. By this time, with AMERICA resting day after day at anchor in front of the clubhouse, occasionally going out for a solitary day sail, England was showdown-mad.

The *Times* of London published a scathing article denouncing the bad sportsmanship of the visitors' British hosts and shamed the Royal Yacht Squadron into allowing the schooner to sail in one of its events. John C. Stevens decided to race for the Hundred Guinea Cup, a risky event heavily favoring local knowledge of currents and obstacles.

The race began at 1000 on August 22, 1851, with the yachts anchored in two rows for the start. Of 18 boats entered, 15 showed up at the line. These ranged in size from the 392-ton BRILLIANT to the 47-ton AURORA. AMERICA was the last boat to start either intentionally "to give others a start, so as not to get crowded amongst them, and to pass them where she liked when she got fairly off," or unintentionally because she was overriding her anchor. But to the amazement of all, AMERICA relentlessly worked her way through the fleet, and finally took the lead.

AMERICA crossed the finish line at 2037; AURORA, the second boat to finish, crossed at 2045. As AMERICA dipped her colors in salute to the king and queen aboard the royal yacht VICTORIA AND ALBERT, the 132-year tradition had begun.

George Steers

The man who was to become "the beacon in the history of American shipbuilding" was born in 1819. George Steers was the son of an English shipwright who moved his family to America from Devonshire. A young mathematical genius, George went to public school and helped in the boat shop where his father built small, fast craft for the gentleman yachtsmen of the day.

We know that he was acquainted with John Cox Stevens's family when he was a young man; at the age of 18, Steers designed a racing rowboat named the JOHN C. STEVENS. By 1838, he was creating the boats whose names are the cornerstones of the history of American yacht design. To name a few: GIMCRACK, CYGNET, SYBIL, UNA, SIREN, CORNELIA, SILVIE, JULIA, HAZE and AMERICA.

The nine-foot golden eagle on AMERICA's stern went with the yacht when she was sold in the fall of 1851. Removed from the transom years later while the boat was undergoing repairs at Nicholson's in Gosport, England, it was eventually recovered from its position over the entrance of the Eagle Hotel on the Isle of Wight. The eagle was returned to the New York Yacht Club in 1912, where it is on permanent display in the Club House lobby.

This 1851 chromolithograph by Charles T. Rodgers is entitled "American Superiority at the World's Great Fair." AMERICA is surrounded by wondrous examples of American ingenuity and engineering genius, including Palmer's artificial leg, McCormick's reaper and Colt's repeating pistol.

The Queen Pays a Visit

Her Majesty Queen Victoria and the prince consort were received aboard AMERICA the day after the race by Commodore Stevens. Captain Brown, a fastidious boat-keeper, asked Prince Albert to wipe his feet before going below: "I know who you are, but you'll have to wipe your feet," he said. The queen spent half an hour on board. At her request, she was given a thorough tour of the bilges and was shown the way the ballast was stowed. She wiped her lace handkerchief over the shelves of the galley and it came away spotless. Before leaving, she presented a gold sovereign to each crew member.

The next day, Captain Brown received a package from the queen containing a gold pocket compass and a note that read, "Her Majesty hopes he might keep it as

Left to right: AMERICA syndicate member James A. Hamilton, the Prince Consort, Alfred Lord Paget, the queen and Commodore John C. Stevens. Note that AMERICA's tiller has been turned into a wheel, probably for the sake of composition.

bright as he keeps his ship." The queen was said to have been "so impressed with what she saw, and those to whom she spoke, that she became, and remained throughout her long reign, a staunch and powerful ally of the new country."

AMERICA the beautiful has been an inspiration to artists of all persuasions from the moment her legend began on August 22, 1851. The "America Schottisch" was written for John Cox Stevens by William Dressler. Its cover is illustrated with a lithograph of the yacht by Sarony & Major. The scrimshaw of AMERICA was created around 1987 by Robert Spring.

YACHT "AMERICA" FOR SALE.

PARTICULARS.

Tonnage............170⅜⅜
Build............Carvel
Material............Oak and Fir
Age............Launched in 1851 ⎫ See Register,
Breadth of Beam..........22 feet ⎬ 93 feet 6 ins.
Length between Perpendiculars ....⎭
Ditto over all ....102 feet

Height between Decks (Saloon) between beams 6ft. 7⅜ins.
  under 6ft. 3in.: forward 6ft. 1⅜ins. between beams
Draft of water............Fore 6ft. 7ins.: aft 11ft.
Rig............Clipper Schooner, setting one gaff-topsail
Coppered............Copper Fastened
Builder..........Mr. H. WILKES, of New York, America
Where Lying..........Off Hardway, Portsmouth Harbour
Lowest Price........Cash,   Pounds Sterling

INVENTORY, PLANS OF CABINS, &c.

Shortly after winning the Hundred Guinea Cup, AMERICA and her owners parted ways when she was sold to an Irish nobleman for 5,000 pounds. Her memory and accomplishment would last forever on her soon-to-be-a-namesake trophy, right.

THE "AMERICA'S" CUP.

The Club fleet rests in Newport, right, captured in an early 1865 photograph.

An instant affinity sprang to life between Newport, seen above in a Buttersworth painting, and the New York Yacht Club from the moment the first Club fleet arrived on August 5, 1844. The terms New York and Newport Society were soon interchangeable as the season's schedule and the harbor were filled with yachting-related activities. On race days, hundreds of spectator vessels churned their way past Castle Hill to the starting area; the ocean drive was "thronged with carriages and people afoot." Newport Harbor at night was an unforgettable sight; illuminated strings of electric bulbs stretching between yachts' masts gave the harbor a fantastic aura. A social arbiter described the festivities as the "usual extravagant dinners and balls transferred from dry land to palaces that floated." The Club fleet rests in Newport, right, captured in an early 1865 photograph.

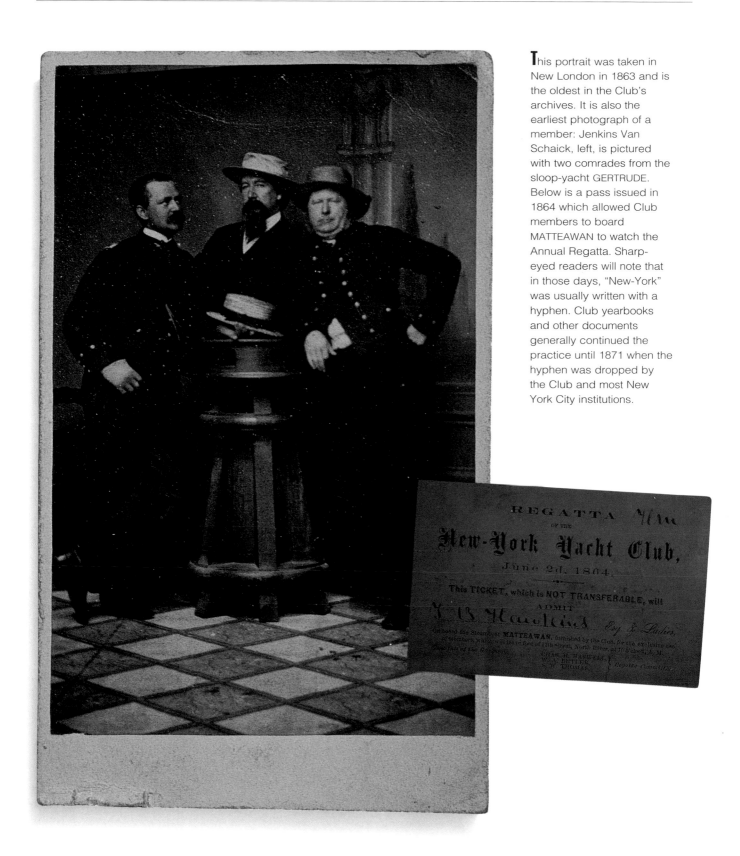

This portrait was taken in New London in 1863 and is the oldest in the Club's archives. It is also the earliest photograph of a member: Jenkins Van Schaick, left, is pictured with two comrades from the sloop-yacht GERTRUDE. Below is a pass issued in 1864 which allowed Club members to board MATTEAWAN to watch the Annual Regatta. Sharp-eyed readers will note that in those days, "New-York" was usually written with a hyphen. Club yearbooks and other documents generally continued the practice until 1871 when the hyphen was dropped by the Club and most New York City institutions.

The Great Transatlantic Race of 1866

The idea to sail this historic race was conceived at a dinner at the Union Club in October 1866. George A. Osgood and Pierre Lorillard, Jr., were discussing the relative merits of their yachts, FLEETWING and VESTA, over an excellent meal washed down by a copious amount of fine wine. The casual pre-dinner boasts became

serious challenges; finally the two men committed their yachts to a December match race from Sandy Hook to the Isle of Wight. Each man wagered $30,000 — winner take all.

Word of the race and the wager soon reached James Gordon Bennett, Jr., the flamboyant son of the immigrant-turned-millionaire publisher of the *New York Herald*, who had been elected a member of the Club at age 16. Bennett and his schooner HENRIETTA were perfectly suited to the desperado nature of a winter transatlantic race. Osgood and Lorillard agreed to let him join the race and the purse was raised to $90,000, a high-stakes sum worth almost $2 million in 1994 dollars.

The race started from New York on the cold afternoon of December 11. James Gordon Bennett was the only owner to make the passage, which was struck by tragedy on December 19 when the yachts ran into gale-force winds and heavy seas. HENRIETTA's Captain Samuels later wrote, "Our staunch little greyhound had but one chance in a thousand to weather such a terrific

gale, but that chance was hers and she came out of it alive. A great sea had boarded us and we did not know whether the vessel would ever come from under it or not. She was in a life and death struggle and only by God's mercy did she win." FLEETWING had similar problems but with direr consequences: six sailors were

Sarony
68c BROADWAY, N. Y.

washed overboard and lost.

The race was won on Christmas Day by HENRIETTA. The log shows her run of 3,105 nautical miles took 13 days, 21 hours and 55 minutes. Bennett would be the only man in the history of the Club to serve twice as Commodore (1871-74 and 1884-85).

The truth or dare nature of the 1866 transatlantic race was a perfect fit for the bravado nature of James Gordon Bennett, above. December in the North Atlantic delivered horrendous winds, snow-storms and perilous seas which almost swamped HENRIETTA, far left. The 1867 painting shows, left to right, HENRIETTA, FLEETWING and VESTA at the start.

THE NEW YORK YACHT CLUB REGATTA.
THE START FROM THE STAKE BOAT IN THE NARROWS,
OFF THE NEW CLUB HOUSE AND GROUNDS. STATEN ISLAND. NEW YORK HARBOR.

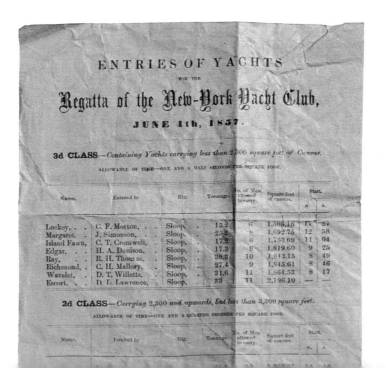

ENTRIES OF YACHTS
FOR THE
Regatta of the New-York Yacht Club,
JUNE 4th, 1857.

3d CLASS—*Containing Yachts carrying less than 2,300 square feet of Canvas.*

ALLOWANCE OF TIME—ONE AND A HALF SECONDS PER SQUARE FOOT.

Name.	Entered by	Rig.	Tonnage.	No. of Men allowed to carry.	Square feet of canvas.	Start. M.	Start. s.
Luckey,	C. F. Morton,	Sloop,	15.2	6	1,504.13	17	27
Margaret,	J. Simonson,	Sloop,	25.2	8	1,692.75	12	58
Island Fawn,	C. T. Cromwell,	Sloop,	17.2	6	1,753.69	11	04
Edgar,	H. A. Denison,	Sloop,	17.3	8	1,819.60	9	25
Ray,	R. H. Thomas,	Sloop,	30.3	10	1,843.15	8	49
Richmond,	C. H. Mallory,	Sloop,	27.4	9	1,845.61	8	46
Wavelet,	D. T. Willetts,	Sloop,	31.6	11	1,864.53	8	17
Escort,	D. D. Lawrence,	Sloop,	33	11	2,196.19	—	—

2d CLASS—*Carrying 2,300 and upwards, but less than 3,300 square feet.*

ALLOWANCE OF TIME—ONE AND A QUARTER SECONDS PER SQUARE FOOT.

Name.	Entered by	Rig.	Tonnage.	No. of Men allowed to carry.	Square feet of canvas.	Start. M.	Start. s.

In 1868, the Club moved to Staten Island where the Annual Regatta included VESTA, HENRIETTA, FLEETWING and other prominent yachts. The Currier & Ives lithograph shows the 10 entries anchored in assigned places before the start with only their aftersails raised. As a starting gun was fired for each yacht according to its handicap, crews scrambled to get the boats underway by hoisting anchors and jibs at the same time. This method of starting races from anchor or moorings was discontinued after the 1870s.

30

Attention to comestibles is a high priority for New York Yacht Club regattas famous for their feasts both visual and tangible, as illustrated in this Bill of Fare. An aspect of the 1859 Regatta reported in the daily press was the fact that the three winning yachts were visitors from Philadelphia. They claimed several particularly handsome food and beverage-oriented Club trophies; "A valuable Tiffany tureen, a punchbowl with handles like the rudder of a Roman galley, a wine cooler, Etruscan in shape, and a covered dish for stewing oysters."

NEW YORK
Yacht Club Regatta.

JUNE 2d, 1859.

BILL OF FARE.

CORNED BEEF.

A LA MODE BEEF.

DO.   VEAL.

SALMON.

LOBSTER SALAD.

CHICKEN   DO.

BONED TURKEY & CHICKEN.

ROASTED CHICKENS.

DO.   PIGEONS.

HAM—TONGUE.

PICKLED OYSTERS.

JELLY.

CHARLOTTE RUSSE.

ICE CREAM.

STRAWBERRIES.

CAKE.

FRUIT.

REGATTA
OF THE
New York Yacht Club
THURSDAY, JUNE 22, 1871.

This Ticket, which is NOT TRANSFERABLE will

Admit _____ Wm H Major Esq. and Ladies,

On board the Steamboat MIDDLETOWN, furnished by the Club for exclusive use of Members, which will leave foot of Desbrosses Street at 10½ A. M.

Show this at the Gangway.

PHILIP SCHUYLER,
STUART M. TAYLOR,   REGATTA COMMITTEE.
WM. BUTLER DUNCAN.

The first home game of the 113-year, 25-match defense of the America's Cup went to MAGIC, seen above on a pre-race sail, by 39 minutes and 17 seconds. The first series was sailed on the Southwest Spit, Sandy Hook Lightship course, on August 8, 1870. A fleet of 15 yachts sailed the 35.1-mile race in which AMERICA, now owned by the U.S. Navy and sailed by midshipmen, finished fourth; the challenger CAMBRIA finished 10th on corrected time. An inscription on the back of this photograph of CAMBRIA, above right, notes that her square sails were not carried in the race for the America's Cup.

At her birth, the motive behind MOHAWK's design was, according to W. P. Stephens, "the great American idea of 'the biggest thing on earth' and 'licking all creation.'" Built in 1875 for Vice Commodore William T. Garner, MOHAWK was nothing if not extreme; 330 tons, 141 feet overall, with a 30-foot, 4-inch beam and 6-foot draft (total draft being 31 feet 5 inches with the board down). Her 28-foot-square main saloon was filled with paintings; the owner's stateroom was 18 by 13 feet and

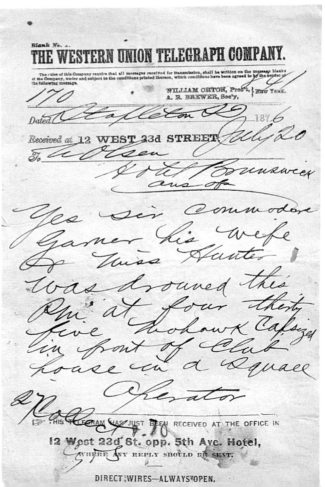

her features included hot and cold running water and steam heat. Indeed, it was suggested that the most important requirement of her design was the enormous size of her saloon. If size, speed and elegance were the parameters of her creation, they were tragic circumstantial factors in what would become the greatest catastrophe in American yachting to that time, an accident that was the result of the confluence of gross carelessness and the yacht's radical design.

On July 20, 1876, MOHAWK was capsized while at anchor by a "Staten Island twister," her mainsail, foresail and both topsails set, as the crew made ready for an afternoon sail. Five people drowned below-decks, including Vice Commodore Garner and his wife. Although MOHAWK survived to serve many years in the service of the Coast and Geodetic Survey, her tragedy that sunny summer afternoon was the demise of the "era of the Great Schooners."

The launching of the 94-foot PURITAN in 1885 marked the dawn of the Edward Burgess era of America's Cup defenders. PURITAN was built for a powerful Boston syndicate managed by General Charles J. Paine and financed by J. Malcolm Forbes, above, both members who felt the Club could not field a strong New York team for the defense. Indeed, a writer for the *Evening Telegram* wrote "it was a good thing that Boston was to build a Cup candidate, as after the trial races she could be used for carrying brick on the Hudson River." Soon after her launching, PURITAN was described as "undoubtedly the fastest American yacht ever built." Her resounding win over FORTUNA for the 1885 Goelet Cup for Sloops, far right, above, clinched her selection as the obvious best choice for the defense. She is seen, far right below, preparing for the trials and above, leading GENESTA in one of the two races of the 1885 America's Cup.

AND—MAY THE BEST BOAT WIN!

Ogden Goelet presented the first Goelet Cup for Schooners, valued at $1,000, and the Goelet Cup for Sloops, valued at $500, at the Club meeting held on February 2, 1882. The trophies were raced for annually until his death aboard his steam yacht MAYFLOWER, off Cowes, England, on August 27, 1897. They were replaced by the Astor Cups, which are still in competition today. The 1886 Goelet Cup for Schooners, above, was won by GRAYLING. It weighs 39 pounds and was fabricated by Tiffany & Co.

Yachting as a spectator sport is depicted in this painting by Julius L. Stewart, who shows the friends of James Gordon Bennett perfecting their technique aboard his 226-foot yacht NAMOUNA. The rigorous demands of the sport were tempered by the permanent staff of 50 and the yacht's guest-friendly accouterments. NAMOUNA's interior was designed by Stanford White and featured Louis Tiffany glass decorations, a dining hall, offices and nine staterooms. In this 1890 painting, James Gordon Bennett is sitting at the left wearing a white suit and the actress Lily Langtry is seated at the right petting her little dog. Her close friend, New York stockbroker Frederic Gebhard, is reading to her. The 1889 engraving, below, is appropriately titled, "Doing the New York Yacht Club Regatta From the Club Boat: A Scene on the Lower Bay."

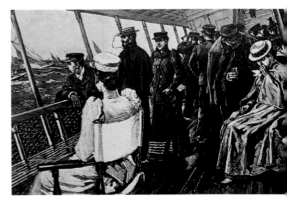

The Man Who Did It All

Nathanael Greene Herreshoff was born in Bristol, Rhode Island, on March 18, 1848. He was an innovator, naval architect, engineer, inventor and brilliant sailor. Over a period of 72 years, he designed more than 2,000 craft and produced more than 18,000 drawings. His son A.G. Herreshoff, writing in 1981, lists some of his father's creations:

- yacht time allowance tables
- the coil boiler with steam separator and superheater
- the dynamometer and technique for testing powerboat hull models
- the instrument to precisely measure offsets from half models made for hull designs
- the form and method of both wood and metal yacht construction
- DEFENDER, the first aluminum-hulled America's Cup defender
- longitudinal framing for hulls
- cross-cut sails
- the design of fine pitch screw threads for strong, light connections
- the fin keel/spade rudder combination
- the telescoping topmast housing
- seven- and fifteen-strand wire rope for low stretch
- the Universal Measurement Rule
- the first folding propeller and first weedless propeller
- below deck winches (first used aboard RELIANCE in 1903)
- the first aluminum spar (DEFENDER's 1895 gaff)
- sail slides and rolled sail tracks
- the method of splicing wire to rope
- the first United States patent on catamaran sailboats
- tacking downwind of yachts
- the modern yacht form with a cutaway profile for low wetted surface

It is in the area of the modern yacht profile that the second turning point in naval architecture occurred, 40 years after the blitz of AMERICA.

The year was 1891 and the boat was GLORIANA.

GLORIANA eats out to weather under the increased sail area and over the lengthened-when-heeled waterline that resulted in her perfect 8-0 racing record and started a whole new look.

Club member Edwin D. Morgan wanted a boat built to race in the popular 46-foot class, and "Captain Nat" was commissioned. The design was as important a milestone in his career as it was in the evolution of speed under sail. If the boat was not fast, "it would be said of him that his forte was the construction of steam craft, and that he would best stick to that branch of marine architecture." GLORIANA was an immediate, consistent, overwhelming success. "Alty" Morgan cleaned up, winning eight of the eight races he entered that season. He then retired the boat from competition in order to give everyone else a chance. GLORIANA was considered the "swiftest and ablest boat of her size on this side of the ocean, if not in the world."

What was it? What had happened? Herreshoff designed GLORIANA to fare well under the then-current "Seawanhaka Rule." To accomplish that, a shortened waterline and lengthened bow equaled a decreased rating. The decreased rating was countered by an increased sail area. The increased sail area was balanced by a deep, ballasted keel. Combine that with the switch from clipper or hollow bow to convex-curved or spoon bow, and the boat was born to heel. When heeled over, the boat sailed on a longer-than-measured waterline. In other words, GLORIANA the rule-beater was designed, as someone said, "to sail on her side."

The Herreshoff era produced many one-design classes. In addition to the 46-footers were the Newport 30-footers in 1896, the Newport one-design 70s in 1900, the NYYC 30-footers in 1905, the 57-footers and the 65-foot class in 1907, the NYYC 50-foot class in 1913 and the NYYC 40-foot one-design class in 1916.

He also enriched Club sailing in many extremely popular, small, one-design classes, many of which continue to provide hotly contested sailing to this day. To name a few: the Herreshoff 12-1/2-footer, the 15-footers, the Fish Class, the Buzzards Bay 18-footer, the Buzzards Bay 25 Class and the S Class, which celebrates its 75th anniversary this year. Nathanael G. Herreshoff also designed the boats that defended the America's Cup six times from 1893-1920. These were: VIGILANT in 1893; DEFENDER in 1895; COLUMBIA in 1899 and 1901; RELIANCE, the largest defender ever, in 1903; and RESOLUTE in 1920.

Throughout his life, he was a close-mouthed and extremely private man who lived in a house with its back to the neighborhood and its windows facing Narragansett Bay. A family man with six children, he worked from before dawn until late evening and often slept at the yard to be closer to his work. His son L. Francis said of him, "He was too busy to be human, but a mechanical genius is not meant to be human." He died on June 2, 1938. The end of the Herreshoff era coincided with the beginning of the end of the world as it had been known.

J. Pierpont Morgan, right, was elected Commodore in February 1897. His 241-foot flagship, CORSAIR II, above, was the second of four yachts of that name the family would own. Shortly after the outbreak of the Spanish-American War in 1898, the U.S. Navy was in need of fast yachts "that could be converted into something resembling warships and could be armed to shoot without blowing out their plating." One of the navy's first choices was CORSAIR II, whose services the Commodore quickly offered. Disappointed that his yachting plans were interrupted, he immediately commissioned a duplicate. Launched in December 1898, CORSAIR III was 302 feet overall (61 feet longer than CORSAIR II), but her profile was so similar that most people didn't notice the difference. An oyster plate with the Club burgee and Morgan's private signal is one of the 1,169 pieces of CORSAIR china given to the Club by the family in 1944.

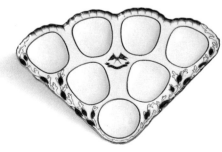

In the third and final race of the 1893 America's Cup challenge by Lord Dunraven, his VALKYRIE II blew out her spinnaker and lost the lead to VIGILANT, as depicted in this Barlow Moore painting. Challenging again in 1895 with VALKYRIE III, Dunraven set a new low in spoilsportsmanship. Following the first race, Dunraven charged the Club with illegally ballasting DEFENDER. Not so, replied syndicate manager C. Oliver Iselin. Following the second race, DEFENDER charged VALKYRIE III with illegally bearing off at the

When Dunraven, left, returned to England, he published a letter accusing the Club of foul play in the 1895 challenge. Following a special inquiry at which his testimony, below, was presented, Iselin and the Club were completely exonerated. Dunraven never apologized, was relieved of his honorary Club membership and was never heard from again. Case closed.

start. Not so, denied Dunraven, but the protest against the challenger was sustained. The third race saw VALKYRIE III cross the line and immediately head for home. DEFENDER sailed the course alone and was awarded the series.

INTERNATIONAL RACES, 1895.

STATEMENT OF LORD DUNRAVEN

—AND—

SOME COMMENTS THEREON.

Did she know something? The Herreshoff-designed DEFENDER, above and right, started life by literally sticking to her ways at her 1895 launching, but was later freed by a flotilla of tugs. As the first keel sloop used in defense of the Cup, her combination bronze, steel and aluminum hull was a revolutionary weight-saving innovation that started self-destructing by corrosion the moment she hit salt water. As a "floating battery," she nevertheless beat Dunraven's VALKYRIE III in the 1895 challenge and lived to serve as a trial horse to COLUMBIA in the 1899 series. Her half-model, right, is in the Model Room.

Defender

Bolles fecit

BROOKL

As portrayed in this painting by Chevalier Eduardo De Martino, the 1899 America's Cup races between COLUMBIA and SHAMROCK attracted an enormous audience. Sir Thomas Lipton's first challenge was a sweet unguent on sailors' souls still smarting from the Dunraven affair. For the first time, in 1899, in the interests of safety and to avoid conflict, the race course was patrolled by six revenue cutters and six torpedo boats. Lipton's yellow-stacked ERIN, J. Pierpont Morgan's black-hulled CORSAIR III and a Fall River Line steamer are seen here in their front-row seats. A brief history of Cup races is told in the souvenir booklet, right.

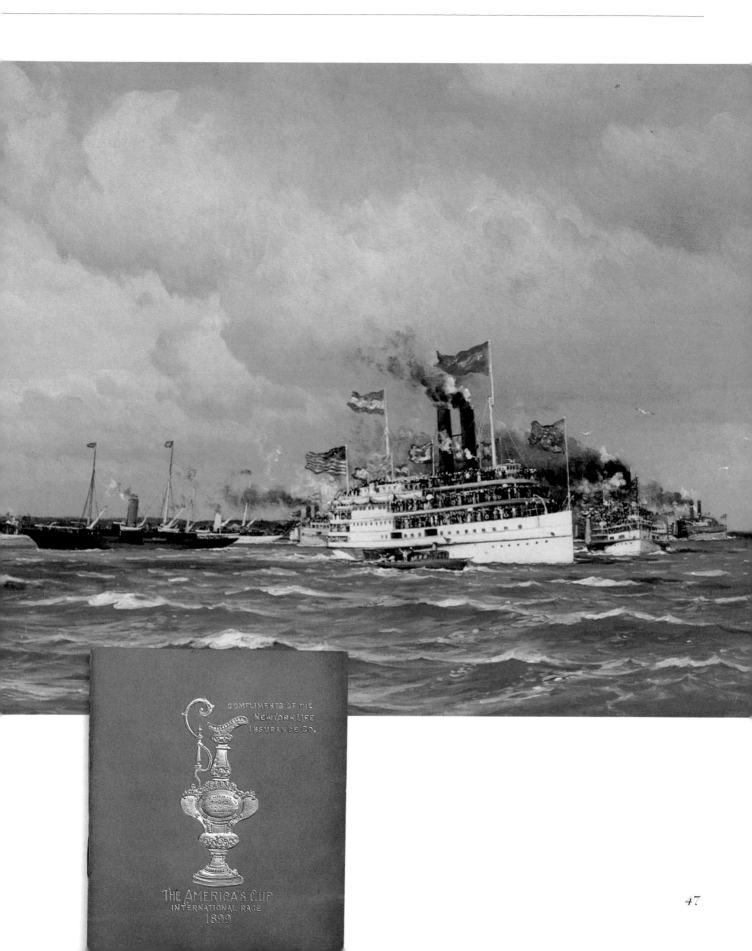

For reasons lost in time, the Staten Island clubhouse was sold in 1871, and meetings moved to rooms on the second floor of a house at 27th and Madison. By 1884, the Club had moved again, this time to 67 Madison Avenue, below, right, where there was room for the Club's growing model collection. The final sentimental meeting at 67 Madison was held on January 15, 1901, and on January 20th, the Club burgee was hoisted at the new 44th Street Club House, right, for the first time.

LAST MEETING IN OLD N.Y.Y.C. HOUSE

Large Attendance to Say Goodby to Madison Avenue Quarters and Hear Reports.

NAVY CUPS PRESENTED

Commodore Lewis Cass Ledyard presided at the special meeting of the New York Yacht Club held last evening at the house, No. 67 Madison avenue. It being the last meeting in the old quarters, there was a large attendance.

Former Commodore E. M. Brown, chairman of the Committee on the New Club House, said that the committee was ready to turn the house over to the House Committee of the club, but was not ready to make its final report. He offered the following resolution:—

Resolved, that on and after this date the House Committee shall have general supervision of the new club house, and shall exercise in reference thereto the power conferred by Article 10 of the constitution; but the committee in the new house is hereby continued for the purpose of enabling them to settle and close their accounts, and to complete any details of construction or equipment.

NAVY CUPS PRESENTED.

Rear Admiral Erben, U. S. N., presented to the club the navy cups before referred to in the HERALD through the following letter to the secretary:—

NEW YORK, January 7, 1901.

... Secretary New York Yacht ...

... member of the ...

The Club Builds a New Home On 44th Street

The general Club meeting in October 1898, began calmly enough. At one point, ex-Commodore Edward M. Brown, chairman of the committee on sites for a new Club House, delivered his report recommending that the Club purchase a three-lot site on West 44th Street for $150,000. The committee further recommended

spending $175,000 to build and furnish a Club House.

To the surprise and utter astonishment of everyone, Commodore J. Pierpont Morgan announced his willingness to buy the land himself and give it to the Club. There had been no previous inkling of his offer. Morgan's two stipulations were that the frontage be increased from 50 feet to 75 feet and the dues increased from $25 to $50. These were quickly agreed to, his offer was accepted and the three lots were soon transferred.

From the seven firms submitting plans for the design of the new Club House, the project was awarded to

Commodore Edward Marsh Brown (1895-96) led the committee that found the 44th Street site; few could have envisioned the splendid building that the Club would call home. The photos show the building in 1901 when a strict rule was broken and ladies were welcomed at the opening. The Club motto, carved over the front door, captures the sailor's desire, "We are carried forward by swelling sails."

Whitney Warren and Charles Devon Wetmore. What differentiated their plans from the others was what won them the commission: the off-center entry, airy two-story entrance hall and, in particular, placement of the Model Room extending the depth rather than the width of the building. These were great exceptions to the architectural rules in vogue in the 1890s. By comparison, most other important clubhouses had a symmetrical facade with the entrance in the middle, a "great room" stretching across the front of the second floor and a formal, grand dining room.

The inspiration of the Warren-Wetmore design was its ship-at-sea echo that is a constant reminder to members of what their building and Club are uniquely about. The Club House's signature features include the shape of the bay windows on 44th Street, the red-carpeted grand staircase ennobled by mementos of the AMERICA, the spectacular display of models and the low-ceilinged Grill Room constructed like the 'tween decks of an old sailing ship,' about which the *New York Times* said in 1906, "Except for the absence of motion one might fancy oneself at sea."

The Best-Known Model Room
In the World

The beginning of the New York Yacht Club's model collection, which now numbers more than 1,200 half-hulls and full-rigged models, can be traced to March 17, 1845. On that day, the rules and regulations of the Club were officially adopted. They had been written by a committee established aboard GIMCRACK at the founding meeting the previous July. Among the rules and regulations was the following: "The model of each yacht shall be deposited with the Recording Secretary before she can enter for the Regatta. The model shall be the property of the Club."

Although incidentally forming the foundation of what is today the largest and most revered collection in the world, the mandatory furnishing of a model was at that time required simply to enable the Club to measure the yacht for handicapping purposes. The minutes of the February 1846 meeting state, "...whenever a yacht is hauled out of water, the owner shall give four days previous notice to the Commodore, in writing, in order that the

model may be obtained." Models were the primary source of measurements in a day before boats were designed on paper.

A uniform scale for models was adopted in 1882 but not enforced until 1905, at which time all nonconforming models were rebuilt and the members charged accordingly. By 1951, the Club relaxed the mandatory requirement to provide a model before a yacht could participate in Club racing. And the tradition continues — the bylaws still in effect today read, "Any member so requested by the Model Committee shall deposit a correct model of his or her yacht with the Club, which shall retain the model in its posession...."

The glorious room that houses the bulk of the Club's model collection is the heart of the Club House. Crowned by a stained-glass skylight, the two-story, 96-foot by 45-foot room has been described as exemplifying the architect's great talents for "creating large rooms of such perfect proportions that a crowd or lone occupant finds them equally inviting and comfortable." Standing America's Cup models are arranged in chronological order so one can walk through the room and witness the living history of yacht design in America.

The Model Room at 67 Madison, far left, and in the early days of the 44th Street Club House, left, were precursors to today's unparalleled collection, above, which consists of more than 1,200 standing and half models. It is a definitive and constant work-in-progress that illustrates the history of yacht design. The Club's collection, originally required for handicapping purposes in a day when yachts were not designed on paper, was listed in this 1901 book, right.

CATALOGUE OF MODELS
THE PROPERTY OF
NEW YORK YACHT CLUB

Not to be removed from the Club House

53

C. Oliver Iselin's wife, shown below in a 1903 *World* Sunday supplement, sailed aboard DEFENDER in the series against VALKYRIE II, on COLUMBIA vs. SHAMROCK and on RELIANCE in Cup races against SHAMROCK III. She was the first woman to sail aboard an American yacht in international competition and traditionally wore a blue and white sailor's outfit with a Club burgee on her hat. The photo, left, shows her seated with her husband in later years.

RELIANCE's career was very dramatic and very brief. Christened on April 12, 1903, the boat was decommissioned 126 days later at City Island, where it was broken up in 1913. Owned by a syndicate headed by Cornelius Vanderbilt and skippered by Charlic Barr, above, the first to defend the Cup in three successive series, RELIANCE's hulking size and radical design invited pejorative description. Called a "skimming dish" and a "damned bronze scow," the Herreshoff-designed sloop was the largest defender ever at 143 feet, 8 inches overall. She carried on a single mast 16,160 square feet of sail, more than any vessel before or since. RELIANCE was so much faster than the challenger that SHAMROCK III not only never won a leg, but was so far behind in the foggy third and last race of the series that it took a tow home and never crossed the finish line.

A month before the 1903 America's Cup races, Sir Thomas Lipton hosted a dinner attended by Clement A. Griscom and other members of the RELIANCE syndicate.

N. Y. YACHT CLUB STATION, NEWPORT, R. I.

56

Stations have been a New York Yacht Club tradition since Elysian Fields and Station No. 1. Club minutes show these facilities were "for the landing and embarking convenience of members and for ships stores, and not for food, drink or sleeping accommodation." Over time, there were 11 stations, all situated along the fleet's east coast racing and cruising route. Station No. 2, first started in 1886, became the East River landing for members who traveled to the city by commuter launch, center. Station No. 3 was in Whitestone, Station No. 4, top, was in New London and Station No. 5 was on Shelter Island. In 1890, the Club acquired property for a clubhouse and wharf on Thames Street in Newport. This site became Station No. 6. It is seen with one of CORSAIR's launches, opposite page, top, and from the water, below. Vineyard Haven became the site of Station No. 7, bottom, in 1892 and was followed shortly thereafter by No. 8 in Atlantic Highlands and No. 9 in Ardsley-on-Hudson. The Glen Cove Station No. 10 was commissioned in 1896 and was heavily used for 52 years. The last station to be built, Station No. 11, was established on Nantucket in 1905 by Club member Paul G. Thebaud, who paid for the building himself.

"And the record still stands..."

The great ocean race of 1905 started from Sandy Hook on May 17. It ended when the schooner ATLANTIC swept past the finish at the Lizard 12 days, 4 hours, 1 minute and 19 seconds later, setting the speed record for a transatlantic crossing by a monohull under sail, a record that still stands today.

The trophy was the ornate, gold German Emperor's Cup given by Kaiser Wilhelm I. The race was sailed without handicap or sail restrictions, the only conditions being that "propellers were to be removed but could be carried on board, and steam power was not to be used in hoisting sails."

The fleet of two British, one German and eight New York Yacht Club yachts was towed to the starting area for the noon gun. They were given a "cheery send-off by all of the spectator's fleet and in particular by a party of the younger members of the Club who chartered a large ocean tug and with a band on board followed the racers and paid each the compliment of playing some of her national airs and giving hearty cheers for each vessel and her owner."

ATLANTIC, named after Brooklyn's Atlantic Yacht Club, was designed by William Gardner and built of steel by Townsend and Downey at Shooters Island, New York, for Club member Wilson Marshall. One hundred eighty-five feet overall, ATLANTIC carried 18,500 square feet of canvas and was sailed by the indomitable Captain Charlie Barr, the foremost racing skipper of the day and three-time America's Cup defender. Marshall and six friends went along as spectators for

GOLDEN CUP FOR ATLANTIC

Yankee Boat Reaches Lizard in Record-Making Time.

TROPHY WON BY THE ATLANTIC.
Designed and Donated by Wilhelm II, Emperor of Germany.

what turned out to be the ride of their (and yachting's) lifetime. Following the great circle route, ATLANTIC logged 341 nautical miles on her fastest day. Her average speed for the 3,014-mile crossing was 10.4 knots.

A decade later, the outbreak of World War I, prevailing anti-German sentiment and the death of his son in the war prompted Wilson Marshall to dispose of the kaiser's cup in a meaningful way. He donated it to an auction that netted the Red Cross $125,000. The winning bidders returned the cup for use at another fund-raiser to be held at the Metropolitan Opera, where it would be demolished by Wilson Marshall before an audience that had paid $5 a ticket to witness the event. As Wilson shattered the supposedly gold cup with a sledgehammer, it fell into pieces and was revealed to be thin gold plate over pewter, worth no more than $35.

In the spring of 1993, a new trophy, the Atlantic Challenge Cup, was donated to the Club. The accompanying deed specifies the challenge is to beat ATLANTIC's elapsed time with a monohull

yacht having similar design characteristics to ATLANTIC. It states, "the intent of the challenge is to produce a faster yacht, using modern materials and technology as well as emphasizing safety and seamanship skills." On May 15, 1993, the 184-foot schooner ADIX sailed transatlantic from Sandy Hook in an attempt to break the record. On May 23, the New York Yacht Club received a communication from ADIX, saying they were becalmed and conceding defeat. And the record still stands.

The 1905 transatlantic fleet encountered a mid-ocean gale during which it is said Captain Charlie Barr squeezed breathtakingly high speeds out of ATLANTIC by refusing to heed owner Wilson Marshall's suggestion that he shorten sail. She is shown, above, during the 1928 race to Spain.

ROBERT E. PEARY, AFTER 23 YEARS SIEGE, REACHES NORTH POLE;
ADDS "THE BIG NAIL" TO NEW YORK YACHT CLUB'S TROPHIES;
DR. COOK TO SUBMIT RECORDS TO UNIVERSITY OF DENMARK

The November 29, 1905, issue of the *Boston Globe*, right, contained the story of the King's Cup, which His Majesty Edward VII presented to the New York Yacht Club in November 1905. It was sailed for annually until 1911. (In 1912, King George V presented the Club with a new King's Cup, to be raced for under the same conditions as the one given by his late father, who had passed away the year before. In 1953, Queen Elizabeth II presented the Club with the Queen's Cup, a perpetual trophy that replaced the King's Cup, which was retired following the death of her father.) On April 6, 1909, Club member Robert E. Peary reached the North Pole. The cable announcing his achievement arrived at the New York Yacht Club five months later on September 6. It read, "Steam Yacht ROOSEVELT, flying Club burgee, has enabled me to add North Pole to Club's other trophies." The phrase "Big Nail" in the article, above, is a translation of the Eskimo term for North Pole.

THE BOSTON GLOBE-NOVEMBER 28.

TROPHY KNOWN AS THE "KING'S CUP"

Presented By King Edward VII---To be Raced for by American Yachts.

NEW YORK, Nov 27—Announcement was made tonight at the New York yacht club of the presentation to the club by King Edward VII of a trophy, to be known as the "King's Cup," and to be raced for annually by American yachts in American waters.

More than a hundred yachtsmen responded to the call for a special meeting of the New York yacht club tonight when Commodore Frederick G. Bourne, who presided, said:

"Some time ago I received an informal and confidential letter from Lord Crawford, informing me that it was his majesty's desire to present a cup to the New York yacht club, to be sailed for annually under terms and conditions to be formulated, and asking my cooperation in order to arrive at a set of rules or regulations which would at the same time carry out his majesty's object and be agreeable to the New York yacht club.

"Thereupon some exchange of communications took place between us, and rules and regulations of the character I have mentioned were formulated, and I have received from Lord Crawford a letter in which he says: 'It is, therefore, my pleasing duty on behalf of his majesty to inform you formally that it is his desire to present a cup to the New York yacht club which shall be competed for annually by yachts belonging to an American yacht club of good standing, subject to the rules and regulations sent.'"

Continuing, the commodore praised the king highly and said that such sug-

2. Races for this cup shall be sailed under the racing rules of the New York Yacht club, as the same shall be from time to time in force, including the rules for measurement and time allowance, except as otherwise provided in these terms and conditions.

4. Any yacht belonging to any yacht club in the United States in good standing shall be eligible to enter in these races, provided that, in the case of a single-masted vessel, she be of a water-line length of not less than 50 feet, and that in the case of a vessel of more than one mast, she shall be of a water-line length of not less than 60 feet, but these limitations of dimensions may be from time to time altered by the unanimous action of the flag officers of the New York Yacht club, taken not less than 10 months prior to the race to which such alteration shall be applicable.

5. The courses and dates and any other conditions, or with the racing rules of the New York Yacht club shall be determined from time to time by the flag officers of that club, but unless circumstances shall arise which in the judgment of the flag officers make it inexpedient to do so, the races shall preferably take place over one of the courses off Newport during the annual squadron cruise of the club.

6. All races for this cup shall be sailed without time limit.

7. Entries for these races must be in writing and must be lodged with the regatta committee of the New York yacht club not later than 48 hours before the time of starting.

Commodore Ledyard offered the following resolutions, a copy of which was cabled to the king:

"The New York yacht club desires to express its sincere

Perceived as belonging to a high-society, big-business, fast-lane world, yachts and the men and women who sail them have always been the larger-than-life stuff caricatures and headlines are made of, as seen in these articles from the Club's collection of scrapbooks.

LAUNCHING
YACHT "ALOHA"
FOR·NEW YORK Y.C.
AT·QUINCY·MASS·1910

Arthur Curtiss James, above, Commodore from 1909 to 1910, was a blue-water sailor who never hit the high seas without all the comforts of home. In 1893, when James was 26, his father gave him the 175-foot schooner CORONET, aboard which he logged over 60,000 miles. Built in 1885, CORONET's interior fittings included "carved mahogany paneling, granite counter tops, a marble staircase and a piano." (Happily, CORONET is alive and well today. One of the oldest yachts still in commission, she is scheduled for total restoration.) ALOHA, left, however, was Arthur Curtiss James's crowning glory and the vehicle for the realization of his lifetime dream of a circum-navigation. Designed by Clinton Crane, she was 216 feet overall and carried a crew of 38. In 1921, James and a party of friends sailed, motorsailed, socialized and golfed their way around the world aboard the sumptuous ALOHA on a 259-day voyage that was pure pleasure for all concerned.

Cornelius Vanderbilt, right, Commodore from 1906 to 1908, and international social and yachting doyen, summered at The Breakers, his family's home in Newport, which Henry James described as "the only place in America where enjoyment is organized." It has been the site of many Club events, including this summer's Sesquicentennial Ball. Part of the nine-boat New York Yacht Club one-design Fifty-Foot fleet is shown, above, racing at Larchmont in 1913. The gaff-rigged sloops were designed and built by Nathanael G. Herreshoff at Bristol and measured 50 feet at the waterline; 72 feet overall.

The World's Greatest Loser

Sir Thomas Johnstone Lipton was born in Glasgow, Scotland, on May 10, 1850, the same year construction began on AMERICA. He was born in poverty to a family that had fled Ireland during the potato famine. Despite the fact that he never had the benefit of formal education, the international commercial empire he created eventually made him one of the richest men in the world.

Sir Thomas was the sole challenger for the America's Cup from 1899 to 1930. Over a course of 31 years, five challenges and five yachts named SHAMROCK (with time out for the world to right itself after World War I), Sir Thomas won only two races. He endeared himself to the American public for his unflagging good sportsmanship and came to be known as "the world's greatest loser."

His first attempt to "lift the ould mug with a green boat" was instigated by his great friend Edward, Prince of Wales, who saw the America's Cup challenge as a way to soothe Anglo-American bitterness following the Dunraven dispute, in which the Club was accused of foul play.

Lipton came to yachting in his late forties after a public offering of the grocery business he had founded in 1890 made him wealthy. He was at first scorned as a landlubber; indeed, he never set foot aboard any SHAMROCK during a race. He was, however, a keen negotiator and a tough opponent in pre-cup battles. Though it found him late in life, yachting was a true love for Lipton, as he wrote for an American magazine:

"Sailing a yacht is of the essence of all sport to me.

Courage and physical fitness are called for, as also are decision and accuracy of judgment. Yacht-racing is more than merely skimming over the white-capped sea; it is an adventurous wrestle with primitive nature and the complete enslaving of her riotous moods...winning or losing, either is thrilling as long as the sport has been fiercely contested, and human endeavor and superior seamanship have won the day — it is one long, breathless pleasure." Yacht racing was front-page international news in the days of Sir Thomas, and the story of the rags-to-riches merchant trying time after time to wrest the America's Cup from its hallowed perch made great copy. The public waited breathlessly for a successful challenge, rooting for the underdog "sweetheart" who was friend alike of "prince and peasant, politicians, pork packers, prize fighters and publicans."

In 1930, when Harold Vanderbilt's technologically advanced ENTERPRISE beat SHAMROCK V in four easy races, Vanderbilt keenly felt America's sorrow for the aging Sir Thomas, who would not live to consummate the promised sixth challenge. "It was a victory so tempered with sadness that it was almost hollow," Vanderbilt said.

Lipton's loss was yet another setback for a nation now locked in the Great Depression. Will Rogers came to the rescue with a letter written to the *New York Times*; "Let everyone send a dollar apiece for a fund to buy a loving cup for Sir Thomas bigger than the one he

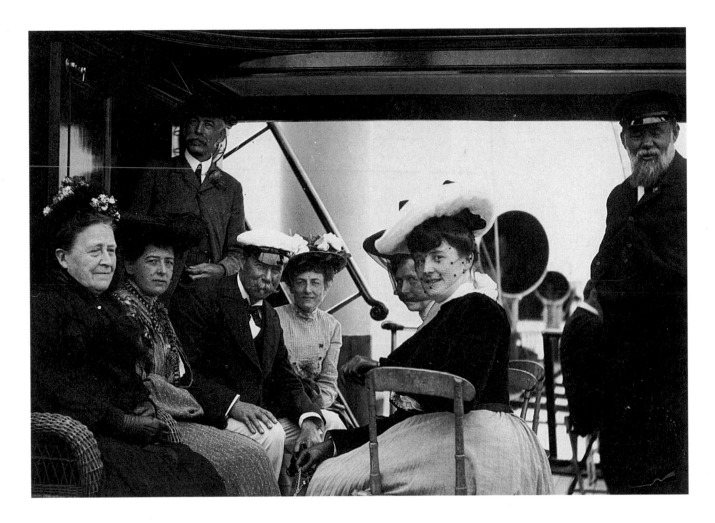

would have got if he had won." Response to this appeal was overwhelming. Contributions, none greater than a dollar and many substantially less, poured in. In under 10 days, more than $16,000 was collected; Tiffany & Co. designed and fabricated an 18-inch-high, 18-carat gilded trophy known as the Lipton Cup. On the four sides of its base are the words "fraternity," "integrity," "courage" and "perseverance."

The gift of the cup was called the "proudest event of Lipton's life." It can be seen today in the Old Glasgow Museum at the People's Palace. Sir Thomas died on October 2, 1931, at age 82.

The *New York Times* said of him in its obituary, "Men will speak of him in superlatives." He was neither just a brilliant businessman nor only a persistent sportsman. When he set out on his America's Cup course, the immediate effect was to soothe enmity

Referred to by Will Rogers as the "World's Greatest Sweetheart," Sir Thomas Lipton is shown here aboard his steam yacht ERIN with Mrs. John Hyslop and her daughters May, Liz and Edith. John Hyslop was elected official Club Measurer in 1886.

between two great nations accustomed to being good friends. After 31 years of failing to arrive at his chosen destination, the sympathy he engendered made him, one of the richest men in the world, a national rallying point for a United States poised on the brink of economic disaster. For that, Sir Thomas Lipton was a gift, indeed.

Sir Thomas Lipton in 1920 with crew members from his fourth America's Cup challenger, SHAMROCK IV. Young Tommy Lipton first voyaged to the United States at age 14. Arriving in New York with $8 in his pocket, he returned to Glasgow four years later with $500 and a head full of marketing ideas which would eventually earn him a fortune.

RESOLUTE's crew, above left, with the yacht's mascot, as they appeared in 1920. The photos, left and on this page, are part of a series in the Club's archives illustrating the moments before, during and after RESOLUTE's dismasting during a 1920 America's Cup trial race off New Haven against VANITIE. The caption of the photo, left, reads, "The RESOLUTE with her rail awash just about five seconds before the accident." The photo above shows the shards of RESOLUTE's mast moments after the dismasting, and the middle photo says, somewhat incongruously, "Bringing in the rescued men back to the RESOLUTE." RESOLUTE was repaired and went on to defend the Cup successfully against SHAMROCK IV.

The 13th challenge for the America's Cup had been scheduled for 1914 but was postponed when war broke out. SHAMROCK IV was actually en route; she continued and was stored in Brooklyn until 1920 when the race was rescheduled. The match pitted SHAMROCK IV against the Herreshoff-designed RESOLUTE, and netted Sir Thomas the only two races he ever won of the 18 he sailed in the course of his five challenges for the Cup. One of the starts is seen, right, from aboard a spectator yacht. Frustration finally got the better of sailing's greatest loser; at the end of the series, he directed the boatyard to "break that boat up; I never want to see her again!" The cedar and mahogany hull was cut into fireplace logs that were used to heat his house for many years.

This speaking trumpet, used by the Race Committee from 1855 to 1865, was discovered in a Club storeroom by Librarian Joseph A. Jackson.

ENTERPRISE, designed by W. Starling Burgess for the 1930 America's Cup defense against SHAMROCK V, was built and launched at the Herreshoff yard in Bristol, Rhode Island, far left. Known as the "mechanical ship," she was belowdecks a stripped-out racing machine full of innovation. In addition to some 20 varieties of winches, her triangular boom was so wide that two men could walk its length abreast; thus, the "Park Avenue" boom, shown left, with C.F. "Bubbles" Havemeyer at the helm. SHAMROCK V never stood a chance. The fourth and final race of the series would be the last act of Thomas Lipton's 31-year quest for the Cup. His words "I canna win, I canna win" were prophetic. He couldn't, and he died before he could challenge a sixth time.

The 1934 America's Cup was the year of the double finesse; Vanderbilt over Sopwith, RAINBOW over ENDEAVOUR. The Starling Burgess-designed RAINBOW was chosen to defend against Sir Thomas Sopwith's ENDEAVOUR, the first newcomer to challenge since 1899. In a six-race match plagued by breakdowns, showdowns and protests, the slower RAINBOW was victorious, and the steelier Vanderbilt never blinked during a series of which he said, "it would seem that errors played the major part in deciding the issue." With her camera and white gloves, Mrs. Sopwith, above, was a constant companion of her husband and one of the few women who played an active role in international yacht racing.

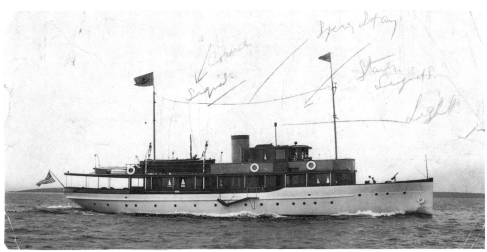

CLOTHO and VALENCIA, above, two of the Club's 20-boat fleet of Sparkman & Stephens-designed Thirty-Two-Footers, built by Nevins in 1936. The making of a proper Race Committee vessel: WILHEMINA, left, being readied for a tour of duty during the 1935 season with hand-written notes regarding proper placement of signal hoists.

This Morris Rosenfeld photograph of the great J-boat fleet was one of Harold S. Vanderbilt's favorites. it shows RANGER in the lead followed by RAINBOW, ENDEAVOUR, ENDEAVOUR II and YANKEE. Her 15,000-square-foot parachute spinnaker was the largest single sail ever used on a yacht. RANGER was the fastest J sloop ever built; in her entire career, she lost only twice in 37 starts, and neither of those was in a match race.

Harold S. Vanderbilt and the Lone RANGER

Harold S. Vanderbilt and W. Starling Burgess were the dream team that produced the successful America's Cup defenders in 1930, 1934 and 1937. Their offspring were ENTERPRISE, RAINBOW and the almighty RANGER, a wonder from its birth that might as well have sailed alone.

When the call came to field a team for the 1937 defense of the Cup, Vanderbilt found himself a syndicate of one as financier, owner, manager and helmsman. He knew to bring the young, brilliant Olin Stephens into the project, and he knew how to talk Starling Burgess into accepting a partner in the design of what would become an instant legend in her own time.

The pairing of Vanderbilt and Burgess was paradoxical. Burgess, a diminutive eccentric, applied a scientific approach to problem-solving. He was a barnstorming pilot who owned Curtis-Wright for a number of years. Anxious to follow in his famous father's footsteps, he was said to do calculus in his head. Vanderbilt was the son of privilege; handsome, tall, a quiet, methodical, conservative man who was also a fierce competitor. Driven by extreme determination, he brought enormous powers of concentration and a penchant for detail to everything he did.

RANGER was the "most revolutionary advance in design in 50 years;" it was the boat that proved the value of tank-testing sailing yachts. One hundred thirty-five feet overall, RANGER completely dominated its rivals both foreign and domestic. Whenever RANGER raced, first place was a given; hot battles for second

The indomitable duo, Harold S. Vanderbilt and W. Starling Burgess, defended the America's Cup from 1930 to 1937 in ENTERPRISE, RAINBOW and RANGER. Although there were a few close calls, the final score of their seven-year career was; Defenders – 12; Challengers – 2.

place came to be seen as wins in the giant's shadow.

The zeitgeist of the J-boats was heady brew the likes of which will not be seen again. As the season of RANGER and ENDEAVOUR II waned, the ominous sounds of Nazi stormtroopers displaced thoughts of racing for the America's Cup in the minds and souls of the world. The cup was sent to the vault at Tiffany's for safekeeping. Sadly, inevitably, RANGER and her fellow sisters were broken up for scrap to help the war effort.

His wondrous J's already dead and recycled, listen to Harold Vanderbilt the poet as he describes his favorite photograph, left, of the brief, shining moment he gave us all: "I like to think of the 'J' fleet as they are pictured.... With outstretched wings, white as snow, they are flying towards us in formation. RANGER, the fastest all-around sailing vessel that has ever been built, heads the cavalcade. Her four older sisters follow in her train. Soaring, a fresh breeze fills the world's largest sail. Presently, their season's work o'er, they will pass by in review. As they have come out of the distance, so shall they go into the distance. The fair wind, their never weary white wings, carry them on — *On the Wind's Highway*, 'homeward bound for orders' — on, to destiny."

Sir Thomas and Mrs.
Sopwith returned for a
second America's Cup
challenge in 1937 with
the Charles Nicholson-
designed ENDEAVOUR II.
Their opponent was the
RANGER team of Burgess,
Stephens and Vanderbilt,
and they never came close
to winning even a leg.

110 N. Y. Y. C. Members in the Armed Forces

2 of 132 Yachts in Service Have Been Lost in Action Against Enemy Forces

By Fred Hawthorne

Drake H. Sparkman of the race committee of the New York Yacht Club gave out some interesting facts and figures the other day illustrating the important and patriotic part the country's most prominent yacht club and its membership are playing in the war.

It has not been known until now that of a total active membership of 550, the club boasts of 110 men in some branch of the armed forces. Two have received official decorations, and one member, Ensign William B. Lovering, ...tionally known as a

Hundreds of Club members served on active duty in World War II; many yachts belonging to members were enrolled in the U.S. Coast Guard and U.S. Navy during the war years.

79

1945-1983

The Hundred Guinea Cup was, in fact, a bottomless ewer that was 27 inches high and had a girth of 24 inches. The 134-ounce America's Cup resided in its place of glory in the New York Yacht Club for 132 years.

*M*y lifelong fascination with the America's Cup began when, as a young boy, I sailed my flat-bottomed, cat-rigged skiff across Long Island Sound and watched seven J-Boats roar past on the New York Yacht Club Cruise. Commodore Harold S. Vanderbilt's brilliant defenses of the America's Cup intensified my interest and stimulated me to study his organizational and tactical methods, particularly his pre-start maneuvers. I am very proud of the fact that he and I are the only two Commodores to have defended the America's Cup.

Thousands of us returned from World War II with the pent-up desire to resume and extend our sailing activities. Technological advances such as the development of fiberglass for the production building of smaller, faster boats, together with a new, egalitarian sense about sailing, greatly enhanced its accessibility.

Rejuvenated and reformatted after a 21-year hiatus, the 1958 America's Cup was sailed for the first time in 12 Metres. My participation in this dramatic, worldwide event began when I sailed Vanderbilt's VIM in the 1958 trials. I was thrilled to participate in the subsequent WEATHERLY and INTREPID campaigns, both of which were successful

This painting of the 1958 America's Cup Trials by Charles Lundgren is set into an oval molding above the bridgedeck elevator. The oval motif is repeated often in the architectural details of the Club House. It has been suggested that the oval accommodates the inherent difficulty of framing the shape of a sailing vessel, where both height and width are required.

thanks to outstanding designs and outstanding crews. My personal pleasure was enhanced by the fact that these crews were entirely Corinthian, a practice I am sorry to see substantially abandoned.

The America's Cup was lost in 1983 due to a design breakthrough. The exciting, new America's Cup class was born of the realization that the last increment of speed had been gleaned from the 12 Metre design. It is to be hoped that matters of its cost, venue and organization will be managed in such a way that its future is assured.

— Emil "Bus" Mosbacher, Jr.

The staying power of NIÑA's Marconi rig confounded skeptics from the moment she appeared at the starting line of the 1928 transatlantic race to Spain. Not only did the 72-foot mainmast look scrawny, its hollow construction and myriad stays didn't seem beefy enough for the ocean passages she was designed for. Wrong. NIÑA and her rig endure today.

An Affair to Remember

There is nothing usual about NIÑA — not her name, nor her rig, nor her profile, nor her reason for being, nor her accomplishments, nor her remarkable life span (this year marks her 66th birthday).

In 1928, King Alphonso of Spain presented two trophies for an ocean race from Sandy Hook to Santander, Spain. The New York Yacht Club would sponsor and start the race, which was to be sailed in two divisions. Small boats would sail for the Queen's Cup and start on June 30; larger boats with waterline lengths of 55 feet or more would compete for the King's Cup and start on July 7. There had not been a transatlantic race since 1905, and there had never been one sailed in small yachts by amateur crews.

New York Yacht Club member Paul L. Hammond commissioned W. Starling Burgess to design a yacht for the race. His creation was startling; 59 feet overall, sporting a staysail schooner rig decried as a "two-masted cutter," and featuring a 72-foot, pencil-thin hollow mainmast.

And her name? To highlight the Spanishness of the whole affair, two other yachts in the fleet were renamed SANTA MARIA and PINTA. Holà, NIÑA.

NIÑA dealt the world her first surprise by winning the race. Among others, she was sailing against the indomitable ATLANTIC, who was heavily favored. The welcoming party, which included the king, had been scanning the horizon for days anticipating the arrival of a long, black, three-sticked shape. Incredulity reigned when they saw it was NIÑA, the smallest boat in the fleet, who would cross first. The king was ecstatic. Waving his hat in the air from the deck of his launch, he shouted, "Well-sailed NIÑA! I congratulate you. I am the King of Spain." NIÑA then crossed the English Channel to win the 1928 Fastnet, becoming the first American yacht to do so.

Eventually retired for a few years, NIÑA was for sale and in bad shape when Bobby Somerset, former commodore of the RORC, bought her in 1933. Deciding her state of deterioration was more than he wanted to deal with, she was soon hauled and sold.

NIÑA's lucky star re-ascended in 1935, when she was purchased by DeCoursey Fales, left, who would serve as Commodore of the New York Yacht Club and make her his flagship from 1946 to 1948. Their meeting was fortuitous for both. The yacht was urgently in need of a good home, and Fales had found the object of love, devotion and skill that would enshrine them both forever in the hearts of yachtsmen.

Over a period of years, NIÑA was slowly restored and upgraded. Their first major win was the 1939 Astor Cup, which they won again in 1940. It was just the beginning. An Edlu Trophy here, a Cygnet Cup there. A glance through Club archives shows them to be the top team in Cruise squadron runs throughout their career together. In 1941, the pair won the 238-mile Stamford-Vineyard Race, which they made their own for the next 20 years. They would win it five more times, in 1947, 1952, 1953, 1954 and 1960, a record that stands today. They won the Bermuda Race in 1956 and 1962. NIÑA was halfway to Bermuda in the 1966 race without her champion when word arrived that he had passed away.

While NIÑA was once the smallest boat in a fleet of large ocean-racing yachts, those boats were out-designed by the changing rule. By the end of her career, she was a large racing boat in a fleet of smaller rivals. DeCoursey Fales and NIÑA disregarded the vagaries of yacht handicapping systems to which they were so often the winning exception. Continuing modernization kept NIÑA current through decades of improving technology.

After the death of DeCoursey Fales, NIÑA was given to the U.S. Merchant Marine Academy. She passed into private ownership in 1972 and can still be seen, easily identifiable from afar, plying charter-route waters.

BOLERO and John Nicholas Brown. These two names are synonymous with each other and with the New York Yacht Club. Designed by Olin Stephens in 1949, BOLERO burst on a yachting scene long denied its pleasures by the war years and had a long and distinguished career. The 73-foot, 6-inch yawl was the splendid archetype of the CCA Rule to which she was built: fast, beautiful and successful. She is seen, above, on the 1953 Annapolis to Newport race with Commodore Brown at the helm and, right, on the 1954 Annual Cruise.

How the 12 Metres Became an America's Cup Class

The first 12 Metre, HEATHERBELL, was designed and built in England in 1907. The 12 Metre class didn't become popular in the United States until the late 1920s, when six were built as a one-design fleet by Abeking & Rasmussen for American owners. Their popularity increased until the onset of World War II. The class derives its name from an International Measurement Rule; a formula is applied to the boat's length, girth, sail area and freeboard, and the result must be a constant 39.37 feet, or 12 metres.

All remained quiet on the America's Cup front from 1937 until 1956, when Commodore Henry Sears reported that the Royal Yacht Squadron had expressed interest in challenging for the cup in an International Rule 12 Metre. By then, the tremendous cost of J-boats had eliminated them as an America's Cup class, and the Club agreed that 12 Metres were well suited to the job. The only hurdle to overcome was making two changes to the Deed of Gift.

The first would "allow competition between yachts of a minimum 44-foot waterline length, in contrast to the previously required length of 65 feet," and the second would relieve challengers of the requirement that they sail to the United States on their own bottoms. The New York State Supreme Court approved a petition containing these changes to the Deed on December 17, 1956, allowing the Club to "accept challenges and race for the Cup in Twelve Metre boats."

America's Cup, yes, but what a difference! After a 21-year hiatus, the 1958 version of the defense was the first episode in the 12 Metre saga that would last until 1987. Shown right foreground with SCEPTRE, at the start of the first race of the 1958 series, COLUMBIA, designed by Olin Stephens and sailed by Briggs Cunningham, is still considered by many to be the most beautiful 12 Metre ever. SCEPTRE, designed by David Boyd and skippered by Graham Mann, was defeated in a four-race series.

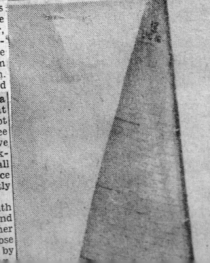

Columbia Trounces Sceptre in 2d Race

Victory Margin 11 Min. 42 Sec.

3d America's Cup Test Today; Many More Spectators Leave

By Bill Wallace

N. Y. HERALD TRIBUNE

NEWPORT, R. I., Sept. 24.—They might as well have carried Sceptre out on a shield today after Columbia gave the British yacht a merciless beating in the second America's Cup The margin in distance was a mile and a half, in time

at the start today. He tailed his foe to within 30 seconds of the gun in the approved manner, and was so good at it that Columbia's men might have thought they were racing Vim and Bus Mosbacher again. Then, with a good safe leeward position, Mann's timing was a bit off and he dropped his boat too far back so he could not pinch up under Columbia's lee bow. From there he might have caused real trouble by back-winding the defender. All in all it was a good start, but the race fell completely apart shortly thereafter.

Sceptre just cannot stay with Columbia sailing upwind, and within ten minutes the winner had a nice fat lead. Then those Britons practically conceded by

The Defense Never Rests

Emil "Bus" Mosbacher, Jr., 39th Commodore of the New York Yacht Club, began his sailing career at the age of five. He has won in small boats, medium-sized boats, big boats and the fairest of them all, INTREPID.

His first racing boat was a Star and, at age 10, he won the first race he sailed in it. At age 18, he joined Cornelius Shield's International Dinghy team. He won the sailing championships at Dartmouth College in 1941 and 1942. Following time out for World War II and business, Bus returned to competitive sailing in 1949 and won the Amorita Cup in Bermuda in an International One-Design and, the same year, the British-American Cup at Cowes in a 6 Metre. He later campaigned his International One-Design SUSAN to eight consecutive season championships.

After a 21-year hiatus, the 1958 reprise of the America's Cup was contested for the first time in 12 Metres. Bus Mosbacher sailed VIM in the cliffhanger defender trials that were eventually won by COLUMBIA. He skippered WEATHERLY to a 4-1 victory over GRETEL in 1962 and drove Olin Stephens's masterpiece, the innovative, revolutionary INTREPID, in a rout of DAME PATTIE in 1967.

Harold Vanderbilt was Mosbacher's mentor, and Bus based his 12 Metre campaign organization and crew training on lessons learned from studying his hero's writings and ways. In *Defending the America's Cup*, by Robert Carrick and Stanley Rosenfeld, Bus echoes Vanderbilt's writings about the RANGER campaign:

"We believe in being on time and in having people in specific places executing orderly, planned routines. I have never made a specific time-and-motion study of the way we planned things on INTREPID, but, in essence, that's what you do when you set up an operation for a 12-Metre boat — you might call it the choreography of racing. You have X number of men who have to do certain jobs with split-second timing. They must do them as fast and as well as possible to eliminate any chance of a foul-up. Organizing, first the physical layout and then the people, is a fascinating study."

Bus made famous the pre-start, tight circling maneuvers that covered and harassed the opponent, often forcing error. It's yet another lesson from the master who, Bus says, "did something like that in the J-boats." Bus Mosbacher has witnessed the entire saga of the New York Yacht Club's 12 Metre chapter of the America's Cup from the inside, as well. Vice-Commodore and a member of the America's Cup Committee in 1983, the one layday he did not play his traditional golf game with Dennis Conner was the day before the portentous seventh race. Did it matter? Who knows?

Two years ago he sailed INTREPID in the 25th reunion of the 1967 campaign. Commenting on the ways of the sailing world today, Bus Mosbacher casts a hearty vote for the fun, amateur days gone by. "I'm lucky I was able to sail when racing was Corinthian. It will always be a wonderful sport; it's just different."

The 1958 defender trials, sailed in the new America's Cup 12 Metre class, were pure excitement. VIM, designed by Olin Stephens 20 years earlier for Harold Vanderbilt and skippered by Bus Mosbacher, gave COLUMBIA, WEATHERLY and EASTERNER a run for their money in a summer-long series of big-boat match racing at its finest. COLUMBIA became the eventual defender.

WEATHERLY, designed by Philip Rhodes for the 1958 defense, finally had her way in 1962 under the command of Bus Mosbacher, foreground. Although GRETEL, designed by Alan Payne and sailed by Jock Sturrock, managed to win the second race of the series when WEATHERLY's spinnaker pole broke, Mosbacher's drill-team campaign, based on his mentor Harold Vanderbilt's method of attack, left little to the imagination.

You Can Take the Man Out of the Office.... Those who serve must be properly dressed for duty, as was the 1964 Race Committee boat ALICIA, left. But how does the Race Committee manage its identical uniforms, day after day? The answer is a memo circulated to the Committee known as an ALL COM which specifies quotidian dress in code flags; "Whiskey Lima" for long white trousers, "Romeo Sierra" for red shorts, etc. So much for the bottoms. The tops come from the chapter of the yearbook entitled "Uniforms and Dress."

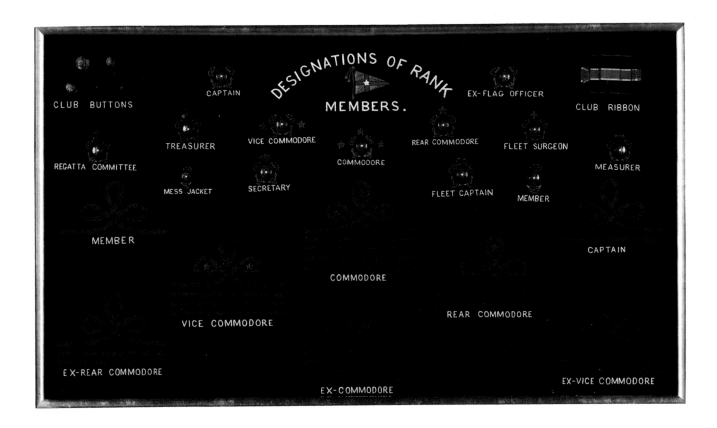

Pictured, left, aboard Commodore Chauncey Stillman's flagship WESTERLY, a 79-foot Sparkman & Stephens–designed auxiliary ketch, are, top row, left to right, Captain Sewall, F. Briggs Dalzell and J. Burr Bartram, Jr.; bottom row, left to right, Willis Fanning, Comdr. Richard J. Dermody, E. Jared Bliss, Harry Anderson, Jr., and Robert H. Wessmann.

The display, above, hangs in the third-floor hallway of the 44th Street Club House. This gentleman's protest set of miniature boats and bouys, which can indicate marks, wind direction and tide, was given to Walter Gubelmann by the family of the King of Norway.

The 1964 America's Cup races between CONSTELLATION and SOVEREIGN were an anticlimax following the defender selection trials that took place between the Olin Stephens-designed CONSTELLATION and the A. E. Luders, Jr.,-designed AMERICAN EAGLE. This photograph of CONSTELLATION is famous for its timing. Taken on the Annual Cruise run from New London to Block Island during a 30-knot easterly, it shows Rod Stephens looking up at the rigging moments before the mast let go. The next day's race from Block Island to Newport was canceled because of high winds. Thanks to that cancellation and high-speed stepping of a new mast, CONSTELLATION didn't miss a race on the 1964 Cruise. The medallion, above, was struck to commemorate Constellation's 1964 defense against SOVEREIGN.

Twentieth-Century Unlimited

I t is not always easy to spot Olin Stephens. Bespectacled and quietly focused on the job at hand, he is an unassuming presence in a crowd. But look closely — there — in the cockpit of the sleek DORADE, the handsome Stephens brothers, Olin and Rod, off on their great circle route to history.

Look again at the young man standing with Harold Vanderbilt on the afterdeck of the wondrous J-boat he helped design at age 24. And again, as COLUMBIA swept the America's Cup into a new era, he who had designed 12 Metres 20 years before. Just look at INTREPID. Look on the bridge of COURAGEOUS's tender, others talking, he with a pair of binoculars trained on the proceedings afloat.

Look at the pages of decades of yachting magazines from around the world, peppered with designs from his table. Look at the records of ocean races and yacht club events throughout our lifetimes, filled with year after year of his winning designs. Look at the generations of children who went for their first sail in an Interclub dinghy, moved into Blue Jays, graduated to Lightnings and were hooked forever.

Look at the IOR rule to which he was a prime contributor, the rule that gave this century glorious racing machines. Look at the list of production sailboats, Dolphins, Weekenders, Nevins 40s, Chris-Crafts, Shields, Pilots, Swans, Tartans and Baltics that give thousands of sailors the thrill of taking to the water and sailing however they choose. This quiet man is twentieth-century naval architecture. And he figured it all out all by himself.

R od Stephens is as famous for his squeezebox musicales as Olin is for his two masterpieces, shown here in photos taken 30 years apart; aboard RANGER with Harold and Gertrude Vanderbilt in 1937, below, and on the stern of INTREPID in 1967, right.

As a boy, Olin Stephens learned sailing "all on his own and by reading everything he could." There was nothing organized about it. When his family rented a house on the Vineyard, he spent the summers in a little boat that didn't fit into any class, sailing out, greeting other sailboats he came across, sailing back in, sailing around, sailing, sailing, sailing.

Time came to go to college. Olin headed to MIT but soon realized it wasn't the place for him then; he was ready to start work. Olin says the single best stroke of luck he ever had was meeting Kenneth Davidson, who worked at the Stevens Institute of Technology. Olin's lucky strike was the experience he gained by starting in with somebody who was working out problems and the testing of small models almost from scratch.

When talk turns to the present, Olin is sorry about the curve of professionalism which has so completely changed the nature of many things, including sailing. Professionalism surrounds us, and he attributes a good part of the blame to television. Insofar as it involves the world of sailing, he hopes the problem will resolve itself by a natural distinction. The people who want to race will hopefully get together in a spontaneous, Corinthian fashion. Hopefully, they will go sailing and have great fun. That would be his most fervent wish.

INTREPID
NEW YORK

"If She Is Right, We Must All Be Wrong"

From the moment the Marquis of Anglesey first laid eyes on the AMERICA and uttered the above words in dismay, boats designed to race for the America's Cup have set the yachting world on its ear. As it was in the beginning, so it continued in 1967 with INTREPID.

INTREPID was a true state-of-the-art spin on the 12's Commandment. Her credentials were impeccable: syndicate by Strawbridge; shape by Stephens; structure by Minneford's; and skippering by Mosbacher.

INTREPID was a study in synergism, as seen in her four major design breakthroughs. Underwater, most apparent was the debut of the spade rudder, a rudder separated from the keel. Next was the fact that there were in reality two rudders — the separate steering rudder, and a trimming rudder on the aft end of the fin keel, called a trim tab. The interaction of these two devices made possible a reduction in the size of the steering rudder, which produced a reduced wetted surface. When the two rudders were set to work together, INTREPID could turn on a dime. Set against one another, the skipper could put on the brakes when and where he wanted.

Topsides, the winches and their accompanying manpower were moved below deck, where they had not been seen since their 1930 placement on ENTERPRISE. Next, the boom was lowered on INTREPID. As Olin describes it in *Defending the America's Cup*, "If you can put your boom down so that the deck serves as sort of an end plate, it has the effect of virtually doubling the

For 150 years, the Club has been a driving force in increasing hull speed over and through the water. During the 1967 INTREPID campaign, above, more than $30,000 was spent on tank-testing hull models at the Stevens Institute of Technology, left. The Hoboken, New Jersey, school was endowed by and is on land given to the school by the family of founding Commodore John Cox Stevens.

deck-sweeping boom. INTREPID's long list of innovations also featured two large foredeck hatches to facilitate sail-handling and a titanium-topped mast with unprecedented bendability.

INTREPID the invincible took no prisoners. Each race, sailed with drill-team precision, was over in the first 10 minutes. INTREPID never lost a leg in any selection trials or in the 1967 America's Cup defense series against DAME PATTIE.

aspect ratio of the sail." There were other advantages to the combination of the above two events. Not only was the considerable weight of the crew and gear better located low in the boat, the absence of their bodies on deck gave the helmsman an uncluttered view forward and lessened the chance of their being injured by the

INTREPID
SPECIAL
GUEST PASS

A non-transferable Special Guest Pass issued to
Robert G. Stone, Jr.
for entrance to all security areas.

By

№ 051

Bus Mosbacher, above, surveying his INTREPID crew and, right, toasting Olin Stephens at the end of the selection trials with Bob McCullough, Buddy Bombard , David Rockefeller and others looking on. Bus and Olin shared their recipes for success throughout the 1967 summer of INTREPID. One of their favorite formulas was an Awful Awful®, a particularly thick milkshake which they drank the night before the first race. The first race won, they reenacted their winning recipe every night before a race and easily beat DAME PATTIE, left, in four straight races.

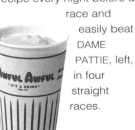

George R. Hinman, left, Commodore from 1959-1960, successfully campaigned a series of yachts named SAGOLA. He is shown, left, at the helm of WEATHERLY during the 1970 defender trials. Although Baron Marcel Bich's four challenges in 1970, 1974, 1977 and 1980 never made it past the semifinals, his campaigns for the America's Cup overflowed with panache. For many years, his home base while in Newport was his 150-foot schooner SHENANDOAH. Bich, above, was an excellent sailor who loved steering his series of 12 Metres named FRANCE. At the helm, Bich was always splendidly dressed in a double-breasted white gabardine suit.

An unusual double-billing aboard COURAGEOUS during the 1974 America's Cup featured Dennis Conner as starting helmsman and Ted Hood, above, as upwind driver. COURAGEOUS defeated SOUTHERN CROSS handily in a four-race series.

THE AMERICA'S CUP 1974

First featured by Commodore Henry S. Morgan to protect his sensitive skin, the "Straw Hats" were worn as a snappy sartorial sunscreen by the America's Cup Committees beginning in 1958. Arthur Knapp photographed the 1977 America's Cup Committee, above; left to right, Clayton Ewing, Commodore Robert W. McCullough, Vice Commodore Henry H. Anderson, Jr., George R. Hinman, Robert N. Bavier, Jr., Briggs S. Cunningham, James Michael and Emil Mosbacher, Jr.

Ted Turner's unbeatable technique at the helm never left the Cup in doubt once he had been selected to defend in the 1977 series that pitted COURAGEOUS against AUSTRALIA, right. His "Captain Outrageous" behavior ashore, however, was a summer-long show that divided his personal observers into two distinct camps of doubters and disciples.

Yacht-Racing Handicapping Systems

Time allowances are an endemic part of sailboat racing and a subject that is a perpetual source of study, debate, blessings, curses, technical wizardry and arguments. Whatever the current rule, it historically describes a wall of limitation that has a hole just big enough for a rabbit to crawl through. Therein lies the source of inspiration and the opportunity for creative interpretation that results in its constant evolution. By definition, the rule, as Karl Marx said about another subject, "contains the seeds of its own decay."

To date, the Cruising Club of America Rule has had the longest run in the twentieth century. In use from the 1920s, the CCA Rule underwent few changes from the 1930s to the 1950s, when it gradually began to give certain advantages to beamy centerboarders not considered as fast as long-keeled, narrow, deep-drafted vessels. FINISTERRE, designed by Sparkman & Stephens and considered "the first of the modern boats," made it clear with three consecutive Bermuda Race wins (1956, 1958, 1960) that a slightly chubby centerboarder, sailed and equipped properly, could indeed be fast. In its wake, a new breed of comfortable cruiser-racers was developed as family cruising and club racing grew in popularity in the post-World War II era.

The late 1960s saw the first major, modern change in the rules. Interest in international racing was on the increase, as was the obvious incompatibility of the CCA Rule with the RORC (Royal Ocean Racing Club) Rule, then used in Australia and England. Through the aegis of the Offshore Racing Council, committees were formed to define a rule that would work well for International Offshore Racing.

At its inception, the resulting IOR rule seemed to treat existing cruiser-racers reasonably well, but technology was insistent. Displacement, weight aloft, accommodations, hull shape and a wide variety of design features soon were seen to pay heavy levies at the rating toll, and the race was on to lighten up. The 1970s saw the IOR evolve into the rule that produced the fast, efficient, magnificent racing machines of the 1980s. By the early 1980s, however, dissatisfaction with the IOR was growing, primarily among members of the sailing fraternity who wanted a more rounded approach that would provide wholesome, conservative yachts on which they could both win races and cruise.

A USYRU (U.S. Yacht Racing Union) resolution and the efforts of Commodore H. Irving Pratt resulted in an MIT study of the basic factors of yacht speed and how these factors could be reduced to a suitable handicapping formula. It was known early on as the Measurement Handicap System (MHS), which became the International Measurement System (IMS). Gradually the IMS gained favor, and gradually it gained status in the major races.

Today, the IMS Rule is in a constant state of refinement. Technology continues its knock at the door, and memories of the demise of its antecedents are in the air. Indeed, the 1994 Bermuda Race recognized the need to divide the supposedly ultimate dual-purpose yachts into two classes: the IMS cruiser/racer division; and the IMS racing division.

As long as the rule spurs competition, embraces the progress of technology and fosters the advance of creative naval architecture, the sport of sailing will remain dynamic, fascinating and fun. Everything new is old again.

Launched in the fall of 1954, FINISTERRE, left, was a breakthrough Sparkman & Stephens design to the CCA rule whose track record has stood the test of time. Sailed by Carleton Mitchell to an unequaled three Bermuda Race wins, she represented, in his words, "...a presumptuous — but still valid — idea: that in a small package could be combined speed, seaworthiness, and comfort, in something like equal proportions."

Commodore Charles M. Leighton's McCurdy-designed 41-foot, 8-inch sloop WHITECAP, above, was built by Hinckley in 1986. A consistently successful IMS competitor, WHITECAP, formerly DRAGON FIRE, won the Herreshoff Medal in 1986; the Corsair Cup in 1989; the Cygnet Cup in 1986; the 1986, 1987 and 1989 Cumberland Cups; and the U.S. Navy Challenge Cup in 1986 and 1987. Commodore Leighton purchased WHITECAP in 1993 and sailed it to class victory in the 1993 New York Yacht Club Annual Regatta. He has also won the 1993 New York Yacht Club Race Committee Trophy, the Herreshoff Medal in 1993, its class in the 1994 140th Annual Regatta and the 1994 Royal Perth Yacht Club Trophy. Charles A. Robertson's 73-foot IOR sloop CANNONBALL, right, designed in 1987 by German Frers, was campaigned to a silver standard of victories. Among her many victories were the 1988 Newport to Bermuda Race, 1989 Queens Cup, 1988 Herreshoff Medal, 1987 and 1988 Royal Yacht Squadron Trophy, 1987 U.S. Navy Challenge Cup, 1988 Clucas Memorial Trophy, and the 1987 and 1988 Race Committee Trophy.

NEW YORK YACHT CLUB
ANNUAL CRUISE
JULY 28 · AUGUST 6 · 1978

Designed by Doug Peterson, a fleet of 23 New York 40s were molded by New Orleans Marine and constructed by Palmer Johnson in 1978. Nine boats of the new one-design class raced on the 1978 Annual Cruise that went from Newport to Nantucket via Block Island, the Sakonnet River and Martha's Vineyard. Sixteen years later, 10 New York 40s raced in the Sesquicentennial Regatta in some of the most hotly contested fleet racing of the week.

FREEDOM, designed by Olin Stephens and skippered by Dennis Conner, was the last New York Yacht Club 12 Metre to successfully defend the Cup, defeating AUSTRALIA in a five-race series in 1980. At last report, FREEDOM, having spent several neglected years in the corner of a boatyard in southern France, was sold to a real-estate developer who planned to use it for company entertaining.

FREEDOM and AUSTRALIA going at it in 1980, left. Rod Stephens, above, and Arthur Knapp, Jr., right, were key players in the decades-long America's Cup story, and sailed together on RANGER in 1937. Arthur Knapp describes that summer in a letter written in 1988; "My summer on RANGER, as Sail Trimmer, was a glorious one! We had a marvelous, successful, happy and wonderful four months.... I relive every moment frequently and vividly. I have been fortunate enough to have fifty-one more years of great sailing and racing since that summer of 1937, but I can't think of anything that tops it."

The 88th Race for the America's Cup

Comfort Zone Denied

The 88th race for the America's Cup was sailed on Monday, September 26, 1983. LIBERTY, designed by Johan Valentijn and sailed by Dennis Conner, represented the New York Yacht Club. AUSTRALIA II, designed by Ben Lexcen and sailed by John Bertrand, represented a Royal Perth Yacht Club syndicate headed by Alan Bond.

One hundred thirty-two years after AMERICA sailed for the Hundred Guinea Cup, the 25th challenge and defense of the Cup would be decided by the final sudden-death race, as the match was tied at three wins each. At 1255, Race Committee Chairman Wm. H. Dyer Jones, below, ordered the gun fired for the

starting sequence. At 13:05:08 LIBERTY crossed the starting line eight seconds ahead of AUSTRALIA II. LIBERTY led at the first mark by 29 seconds, at the second by 45 seconds, the third by 23 seconds and the fourth by 57 seconds. Opinion about Conner's strategy on the downwind fifth leg is a subject of hot debate to this day. His nightmare realized, AUSTRALIA II charged from behind early in the leg and clearly began to overtake him. Conner reacted by jibing away in search of a private breeze, believing that this was the only tactic that might win the race. It was a valiant but risky bet in defiance of the traditional

1983 Race Committee Chairman Wm. H. Dyer Jones and BLACK KNIGHT, the Goudy & Stevens-built Committee Boat, were front-row witnesses to the maelstrom ashore and afloat throughout the last New York Yacht Club summer of the 12s. When AUSTRALIA II crossed the finish line 41 seconds ahead of LIBERTY in the seventh, sudden-death last race, the gun fired from BLACK KNIGHT was a far-reaching shot whose echo still reverberates throughout the yachting world.

The 1983 America's Cup Committee, left to right; Commodore Robert W. McCullough, James Michael, Victor A. Romagna, Commodore Robert G. Stone, Jr., Robert N. Bavier, Jr., Commodore Henry H. Anderson, Jr., Richard S. Latham, Briggs S. Cunningham, Commodore Donald B. Kipp, Vice-Commodore Emil Mosbacher, Jr., and Stanley Livingston, Jr.. alongside FOX HUNTER II at her Goat Island berth. Left, AUSTRALIA II and LIBERTY going at it in one of Dennis Conner's favorite pre-start circling maneuvers.

wisdom of always covering your opponent when you are ahead. By the time they completed the fifth leg, AUSTRALIA II had made up one minute and 18 seconds and was now 21 seconds ahead — the race was all but lost.

On the final, sixth leg of the race, LIBERTY and AUSTRALIA II tacked 47 times, with AUSTRALIA II covering Conner every inch of the way. AUSTRALIA II crossed the finish line at 1720, 41 seconds ahead of LIBERTY. The comfort zone — that positive mental attitude which helped Conner win races — had been denied.

In accordance with the Deed of Gift, America's Cup was presented to the Royal Perth Yacht Club at 1230 on

AUSTRALIA II's 41-second win of the seventh race of the 25th defense of the America's Cup ended a long summer of controversy for the America's Cup Committee and the longest winning streak in sporting history. The America's Cup was presented to Alan Bond, whose mascot was the Boxing Kangaroo, the following day, September 27, 1983, at Marble House.

September 27, 1983, at Marble House, Newport, Rhode Island. The 1983 Report of the Race Committee of the New York Yacht Club states, "The 25th Match for America's Cup is, of course, historic. This Committee was privileged to be part of and to observe some of the finest match racing. To Dennis Conner and the crew of LIBERTY we offer our pride in the tremendous effort they made on behalf of the Club and to AUSTRALIA II our congratulations on winning the match for the Royal Perth Yacht Club."

This scrimshaw-handled rigging knife depicting the schooner AMERICA, was one of the commemorative items presented to the Club on the occasion of the 25th defense of the America's Cup. AUSTRALIA II and LIBERTY, above, in a picture that tells the story of the thousands of words written about the 1983 loss of the Cup.

The Winged Keel That Made AUSTRALIA II Fly

Throughout the summer of 1983, AUSTRALIA II's shrouded keel was the source of an intense controversy, which the press referred to as "Keelgate." The essence of the dispute was centered around the fact that the New York Yacht Club believed AUSTRALIA II's keel might be illegal under Measurement Instruction 7 of Rule 27. After weeks of considerable debate, the matter was resolved on August 26th, when the Club announced it had accepted an IYRU ruling on the matter that pronounced the keel admissible.

In the book *Upset: Australia Wins the America's Cup*, by Barbara Lloyd and Michael Levitt, AUSTRALIA II's designer, Ben Lexcen (who had changed his name from Bob Miller), describes the keel the night it was unveiled to the world;

"The keel is somewhat shorter than a regular keel; it's what you would call upside down. It's narrower where it leaves the hull, and long at the bottom. So if you had a regular keel on an ordinary yacht and sawed it off and put it back on upside down, that's something similar to our keel.

"It doesn't have a bulb like everyone thinks; it just gets a little thicker at the bottom in accordance with its chord. For about half of its length on the bottom it has protrusions (wings) that stick out on each side; they poke down at about 20 degrees, and they are about a

Immediately upon its return to port following the seventh race, AUSTRALIA II's modesty skirt that had shrouded "The Keel" through months of speculation was shed and a new race was off and running; the race for photo ops. Ben Lexcen was photographed the morning after with his unveiled creation.

meter wide and about two or three meters long. They are made of lead and are very thick and heavy.

"On the back of the very sloping trailing edge is a somewhat narrow trim tab that is faired in with a plastic flexible membrane. This plastic fairing bends and fairs the trim tab into a nice, smooth curve." Ben Lexcen's appendage changed the history and the future of yacht racing.

When AUSTRALIA II crossed the finish line 41 seconds ahead of LIBERTY, the committee boat fired a shot that continues to be heard around the world.

As always, lessons learned from the high-technology world of America's Cup participants filtered through all levels of yacht design and competition. For awhile, winged keels sprouted on sailboats of all sizes, but their popularity was short-lived. In an article by Jay Broze, Ben Lexcen says he received what was to him the ultimate absolution concerning "Keelgate" from Olin Stephens. "Olin said it was innovative and he liked it — that was like a personal blessing from God." Ben Lexcen died in 1988.

1984–1994

A special Sesquicentennial logo was designed to commemorate the founding of the New York Yacht Club 150 years ago.

The New York Yacht Club was forced to face the unthinkable for the first time on Monday, September 26, 1983: its best hadn't been good enough. The endless journey of the spectator fleet back to Newport from the 88th race for the America's Cup was in reality a funeral procession complete with grim faces and a sick feeling in the pit of the collective stomachs of members truly and deeply shocked by what had happened. No living person had ever known the world of the New York Yacht Club without the America's Cup; how could we act and feel now that it was gone except saddened and stunned?

The days and years passed, and in 1987 the Club regrouped for the AMERICA II challenge to regain the Cup from the other side of the world. Although our hopes were dashed in the quarter finals, the Cup returned — but to the other side of the United States.

On another front, kismet appeared later that year and its name was Harbour Court. Now a household word and our house for sailors of all ages, its acquisition and refurbishment were a rallying point that came along at just the right time.

As we celebrate the 150 years of our past, remember that the nine gentlemen who founded the Club that afternoon aboard GIMCRACK did so because they wanted to race sailboats. Today, the New York Yacht Club 18 Metre embodies the big-boat racing traditions of our past in a carefully considered format that will take us "back to the future" of our sport.   — Melissa H. Harrington

Harbour Court is as much a home to the New York Yacht Club today as it was to the Brown family for nearly 85 years. Acquired by the Club in 1987, many of the Brown family's personal belongings and valuable collections are displayed for the enjoyment of members and their guests.

The 39th Thrash to the Onion Patch

The biennial Newport to Bermuda Ocean Race is held under the auspices of the Cruising Club of America and the Royal Bermuda Yacht Club, two clubs with whom the New York Yacht Club shares a long and wonderful history of competition and friendship.

The first Bermuda Race had an inauspicious Gravesend Bay three-boat start, one withdrawal and a two-boat finish in 1906. From then it survived 17 years of near-terminal languishment until its resuscitation in 1923, when Herbert L. Stone, editor of *Yachting* magazine and newly elected second commodore of the recently formed Cruising Club of America, decided it was time for America to go ocean racing again. An unsigned editorial in the January 1923 issue of *Yachting* that smacked of H.L. Stone exhorted red-blooded yachtsmen to hit the high seas; "Let's lift the sport out of the rut it's been in the last ten years and show the world there are still as many men who are willing to race on blue water and stand the gaff of a hard four to five days' drive as there have been in the past, and that the breed of 'wooden ships and iron men' is by no means dead." A fleet of 22 boats started in that 1923 "modern" version of the Bermuda Race, which was won on corrected time by MALABAR IV.

Since 1923, the Bermuda Races have been heavily populated by New York Yacht Club entries and winners; the 635-mile course record was set in 1982 by Marvin L. Green's NIRVANA, which finished that year in 62 hours, 29 minutes and 16 seconds, at an average speed of 10.2 knots. Over the years and to this day, many Club members serve on the Cruising Club's Bermuda Race Committee.

Nineteen hundred ninety-four marked the 39th running of the

Bermuda Race and the 150th anniversary of the Royal Bermuda Yacht Club. This year's fleet consisted of 150 yachts, of which 148 finished. For the first time, the race was sailed under two IMS handicap divisions, Racing and Cruiser/Racer. It also featured a "Grande Voile" class for yachts over 90 feet LOA, a J-44 class, and a Doublehanded Division that attracted 17 entries.

The 1994 Newport to Bermuda Race Lighthouse Trophy for the Cruiser/Racer Division was won by Cruising Club Commodore Kaighn Smith in GAYLARK, sailing in IMS Class 8. CONSPIRACY, owned by Donald M. Elliman, Jr., David K. Elwell, Jr., George R. Hinman, Jr., and Richard S. Werdiger won the Grand Prix Trophy for the Racing Division. New York Yacht Club class winners were: WONDER, owned by Stephen A. Van Dyck, IMS Class 3; TOSCANA, owned by Eric P. Swenson, IMS Class 5; LOOSE CANNON, owned by John G. Dunn, IMS Class 6; and FROYA, owned by William G. Gunther, IMS Class 7. GAMELAN, owned by Robert J. Winchester, won the Cruising (Non-Spinnaker) Division.

1964 BERMUDA RACE

NEWPORT to BERMUDA

Twenty years and a difference of 20 hours' elapsed time separate these two photographs. Crew member Bill Close and Commodore DeCoursey Fales, left, celebrate NIÑA's win of the 1962 Bermuda Race at the Royal Bermuda Yacht Club clubhouse. Her elapsed time was 82 hours, 41 minutes and 34 seconds. NIRVANA, above, Marvin H. Green, Jr.'s 81-foot IOR maxi racer, set the course record which still stands for the 635-mile race in 1982. Her elapsed time was 62 hours, 29 minutes and 16 seconds.

The fleet gets underway at the start, left, of the 27th running of the Newport to Bermuda Ocean Race. The 679-mile 1970 race was won by Richard B. Nye's McCurdy & Rhodes-designed sloop, CARINA.

In 1987 the New York Yacht Club mounted a challenge to regain the America's Cup, won by the Royal Perth Yacht Club in 1983. AMERICA II was designed by Bill Langan and sailed by John Kolius for the New York Yacht Club. She was eliminated in the challenger elimination series sailed in Fremantle, Western Australia. In the last challenge to be sailed in 12 Metre yachts, the America's Cup was won that year by the San Diego Yacht Club, which holds the Cup today. Dennis Conner, sailing STARS AND STRIPES 87, designed by David Pedrick, defeated the Royal Perth Yacht Club defender, KOOKABURRA III, which was designed by Murray and Swarbrick and sailed by Iain Murray. Present at the launching of AMERICA II were Commodore Emil Mosbacher, Jr., Commodore Arthur J. Santry, Jr., Admiral King, Sponsor Julia Santry, an unidentified aide, Mark Edminston, Richard J. DeVos, Charles A. Robertson, an unidentified admiral and William F. Buckley, Jr.

Since acquiring Harbour Court in 1987, the New York Yacht Club has hosted many national and international racing events in waters off Newport for sailors of all ages. The Club's commitment to providing a venue for the fun and challenge of competitive sailing is particularly rewarded when it involves young sailors. Eleven-year-old Scott Renken, right, of the Bay-Waveland Yacht Club, sailed in the 1989 Optimist Nationals held at Harbour Court which the Club also hosted in 1992, above.

Robert W. Hubner's Sparkman & Stephens-designed Swan 48, KATE, which he took delivery of in Pietarsaari, Finland, and cruised through Scandinavia, is shown here on the 1972 Annual Cruise flying its favorite spinnaker, Scarface, the day it won the 1972 Una Cup. KATE won the Una Cup again in 1973 and the 1974 New York Yacht Club Race Committee Trophy.

The 1984 New York Yacht Club/Royal Thames Yacht Club team race for the Nichols Trophy was won by the New York Yacht Club. Pictured racing during the event, which was sailed in Christchurch Bay, England, in Sigma 33's, are: left to right, Owen C. Torrey, Jr.; William H. Dyer Jones; Glen S. Foster, skipper; Daniel J. M. Sullivan, the owner's representative and Colin Foster.

Arthur F.F. Snyder's WELCOME, a copy of a revenue cutter designed in 1815, was built by Concordia in 1975. In addition to making two transatlantic passages, she has participated in many Annual Cruises and has, in her owner's words, "represented the Club well."

Just Like Anyone Else

A hefty page of New York Yacht Club history was turned on May 1, 1896, and the newspapers were full of it the next day. "The First Reception for Women Tendered by the Ancient Organization," headlined the *Tribune*. "Delighted With the Punch and the Dainties That Were Served," blared the *Recorder*.

Four hundred invitations for the New York Yacht Club's unprecedented afternoon reception for ladies had been issued by the Receiving Committee; nearly all were marked "accepted." Under the Club burgee at 67 Madison Avenue flew the international code signal, "You Are Welcome." As described in the *Tribune*, "The entrance to each room was adorned with Easter lilies and smilax; wide-spreading palms hid awkward corners, while streamers and bows of the tri-colored yachting colors floated over all."

The Model Room was crowded early on with ladies standing among the palms. One woman gasped in astonishment as she surveyed the hundreds of bas-relief miniatures of sea-craft above the chairs. "However do you manage to keep the dust off them?" she asked. "Madam, they've been dusted three times today," the officer proudly assured her, "but they're not just like bric-a-brac, you know. They're fast."

A magnificent array of Club trophies graced the table in the middle of the room. "There's the Goelet Cup for Sloops," explained one member. "And is that great silver jug in the middle the one that nearly brought on a war?" asked another guest, remarking on the rose-filled America's Cup.

In fact, an amendment to the constitution on the subject of distaff membership had been drafted early in 1894 in response to an unnamed woman being proposed for membership. The anonymous woman was soon revealed as Mrs. Lucy C. Carnegie, the widow of Thomas W. Carnegie, Andrew's brother. Mrs. Carnegie seemed to be sufficiently qualified — she owned Cumberland Island where she moored a collection of yachts and sailing craft, including the 75-foot steam yacht MISSOE, which was not quite large enough to suit her requirements and was soon to be replaced by the 119-foot steamer DUNGENESS. Reportedly quite keen with both shotgun and rifle, Mrs. Carnegie was elected to a special non-voting membership in May 1894.

Seven years later, in January 1901, the Club House on 44th Street opened amid great fanfare and rave reviews. On the special occasion of its opening, "A strict house rule was broken and ladies were invited to be present, a precedent that was not repeated again for many years."

Thirty-nine years, to be exact. In 1940, members were permitted to invite ladies to dine and use the Model Room on Friday evenings. This seemed to start a trend "that has proved popular and successful in the years since."

In 1984, an amendment to the by-laws allowed women to be admitted as regular members. In 1992, the by-laws were further amended to allow women use of the bar and restaurant facilities at any time during hours of opening.

With or without benefit of yacht club membership, women have always pursued the quest for speed afloat as assiduously as anyone. The ranks of solo circumnavigators, long-distance and fleet racers, offshore powerboat racers, Olympic sailors and day sailors (to name a few), are bolstered by the names of girls who grew up with the desire to spend a good part of their lives afloat, just like anyone else.

WOMEN WHO SAIL YACHTS.

MRS. GOELET, MRS. PARKER AND MRS. GOULD TO TAKE EXAMINATIONS FOR FULL MASTER'S LICENSE.

Mrs. Robert Goelet, Mrs. Charles Thorndyke Parker, formerly Miss Susan De Forest Day, and Mrs. Howard Gould are all planning to appear before the United States Government inspectors in the fall to take the examinations required for full master's license. These women, no longer content to be mere passengers on their own yachts, intend to be able, upon occasion, to take full command of them. All have been graduated from a nautical school. Mrs. Parker, who is known to her officers and men as "Captain" Parker, supplemented her school course with private tuition. She has navigated her yacht, the Scythian, around the West Indies, and her sailing master, Richard-

This 1903 newspaper article featured several prominent Club names; only the prefixes are different.

Now That's a Cookie!

Legend has it that when Sir Thomas Lipton visited the New York Club House in 1930, the year of his last challenge for the America's Cup, he asked for some biscuits to be served with his tea. Short on biscuits, the chef served him ladyfingers and macaroons. After nibbling at a ladyfinger, Sir Thomas politely devoured the plate of macaroons, which he pronounced irresistible.

Although always irresistible, the official investiture of the macaroons did not take place until the early 1960s, when the chef decided to try them out on the Executive Committee. By Executive Order, instant tradition.

At the time, the Club purchased its macaroons from the Napoleon Pastry Shop on 45th Street and Ninth Avenue. When the shop closed in 1975, the owner gave the secret recipe to Chef Lee A. Tyre, Sr., and the macaroons have been produced in-house ever since. Chef Lee has never recorded the recipe in writing, but has confided it to his wife and daughter for safekeeping.

Here are some cookie crumbs:

It's Not What You Do, It's How You Do It: Although there is a magic ingredient in the macaroons, the big secret that makes 'em moist on the inside and crispy on the outside is the way they're put together.

Why You Can Never Get Enough: Chef Lee makes the cookies every other day to insure freshness. When they're gone, they're gone.

So How Many Is A Lot? There are 18 macaroons to a pound. The Club serves seven pounds of cookies daily at lunch and five pounds at dinner. That makes 12 pounds or 216 macaroons a day, 1,080 a week, and 52,920 a year, counting summer vacation but not counting mail order, which is a whole other thing.

Annual Cruise

Annual Cruise, N. Y. Yacht Club, New London Harbor, Conn.

The nine yachtsmen gathered aboard John Cox Stevens's yacht GIMCRACK 150 years ago attended to one other very specific piece of business after they founded the Club: they set the date of Friday, August 2, for the departure of the first Club Cruise — destination: Newport.

The founders' intent was exactly what the Annual Cruise delivers today: a cruise in company with friends and some great racing on the way. That August day in 1844, the "little squadron" of eight yachts rendezvoused at the Battery, beat up the East River and rallied at Whitestone for some trials of speed en route to Newport. Today, the New York Yacht Club Annual Cruise is a stately armada, often 100 boats strong, that proceeds from port to historical port along the northeast seaboard, conducting "trials of speed" for trophies steeped in tradition.

Yachting etiquette is alive and well in the form of serious protocol all around as the New York Yacht Club squadron gets underway each day of the Cruise. The harbor start is the best of yachting's best at their best, and its procedure is nothing if not precise. Each morning, at a prearranged

Member Edward E. Roberts's son, Charles, addressed the postcard at left to his sister Harriet, on the occasion of the 1906 Annual Cruise, which sailed from Glen Cove on August 2, and visited Morris Cove, New London, Newport and Vineyard Haven. The 1993 edition of the Cruise, above, took the fleet to the Fox Islands Thorofare.

time and while at anchor, the flagship hoists the code flags "EK" followed by the two signal flags denoting the harbor destination of the day's run from the starboard yardarm. The flagship then fires two guns. In response, the squadron acknowledges these signals by displaying the answering pennant at the starboard spreader.

The flagship gets underway soon after, followed by the flagships of the Vice and Rear Commodores. These three vessels are followed in order by the Race Committee boat, the auxiliary Race Committee vessels and the Fleet Captain's yacht. The squadron falls in behind. When the defile arrives at the rendezvous for the starting area, the flagship lowers its four code flags

and the fleet lowers their answering pennants. The squadron then awaits the hoist of the course signals for the day's racing from the Race Committee vessel.

The Annual Cruise itinerary goes where the Commodore wishes. In the kinder, gentler days of the America's Cup, the contenders for the defense often raced on the cruise, well aware they were under the binoculars of the Selection Committee. The list of winners of the various trophies awarded for the cruise is a roster of 150 years of the finest competitors the sport has to offer. What could be more fun than a week of great sailing and racing, knowing an evening in a beautiful harbor with the New York Yacht Club fleet lies just over the finish line?

PAULINE, far left, shown before the start of the 1993 Squadron Run to Bar Harbor, is an example of the stately, special breed of yachts that serve Race Committee duty. These vessels must not only be somewhat comfortable while remaining on station for long hours in extreme weather conditions, they must accommodate the Race Committee personnel and the substantial, sophisticated electronic equipment necessary for the precision job of scoring, made complicated by the new International Measurement System (IMS) of handicapping. Layday in Edgartown, left, during the 1983 Annual Cruise featured an extended harbor cruise aboard Sven Hansen's ANITRA. The merrymakers included Sven and Ulla Hansen, Commodore Robert G. Stone, Jr., Bill and Betty Foulk, Thor Ramsing, Vincent Monte-Sano, Chip Loomis, Tom Hovey, John Cunningham, Bruce Nourjian, David Vietor, Karen Hansen, Tina Hansen and Dan Briggs, to name a few.

Harbour Court: Home Away from Home

In the spring of 1987, Charles A. Robertson learned that Harbour Court, the former Newport home of Commodore John Nicholas Brown, was for sale. The next day, he enlisted the support of Commodore Robert G. Stone, Jr., in forming a group called "A Group Partnership," with the endorsement of Commodore Arthur J. Santry, Jr. A Group Partnership, formed with 11 other members of the Club, was created solely to facilitate the acquisition of Harbour Court by the New York Yacht Club. After a short negotiation, the John Nicholas Brown family sold Harbour Court to A Group Partnership on July 30, 1987.

A Group Partnership then made a challenge offer to the Club under which the partnership would donate its $1.3 million interest in Harbour Court to the Club, provided the membership raised an additional $4 million.

On October 13, 1987, the Trustees voted unanimously to accept the challenge offer. A fund-raising committee was formed under the chairmanship of Robert G. Stone, Jr.

In 1958, Commodore John Nicholas Brown gave a cocktail party at Harbour Court in honor of the America's Cup. John Parkinson later wrote that "the trustees thanked Commodore Brown for making his house available to 1,351 persons."

Following eight months of intensive renovation and decoration, overseen by Commodore Frank V. Snyder and Project Manager Charles A. Dana III, Harbour Court was commissioned at 1430 on Friday, June 10, 1988. Nearly 1,500 members and guests attended the unveiling of the refurbished mansion. Also on that day, the Executive Committee unanimously adopted a resolution to acquire Harbour Court from the A Group Partnership.

The impact of Harbour Court on Club life is immeasurable. Newport Harbor is now regularly filled with sailors of all ages taking part in Club events. Every member has the opportunity to survey Newport Harbor over a leisurely drink or meal with the pride of proprietorship. For that, we are all indebted to A Group Partnership.

Owen Smith's Sabre 38 UPBEAT proceeds down Chesapeake Bay shortly after the (rare) downwind start of the 1993 Annapolis to Newport Race, during which Mark H. Mattison served aboard as navigator.

Harry Curtis, above, skippers his 1986 Irwin sloop REDHEAD.

Crew members of Alex Van Rensselaer's CANCAN fly their local colors in Castine, Maine, during the 1992 Annual Cruise. They are from left to right, Steve Collins, Jeanie Miller, Bob Lamkin, Bill Miller, Genny Pearce, Ted Duff, Kiliaen Van Rensselaer, Sallie Van Rensselaer, Alex Van Rensselaer, Gerry Pearce and Peter Gerquest.

The New York Yacht Club's 150th Open Fall Regatta was sailed in New York Harbor and involved more than 50 yachts. The active New York 40 Class included, left to right, CARRONADE, sailed by Rear Commodore Robert L. James, TANIWHA, sailed by Thomas H. Josten and HORNET, sailed by George

W. Carmany III. ACTAEON, left, with owner Earl McMillen III at the helm, passes under the Newport Bridge shortly after her 1994 spring commissioning. The 47-foot wooden motor yacht was built in 1932 by A.C.F.

John R. Bockstoce's 60-foot steel cutter BELVEDERE at anchor in Hornsund, Spitsbergen, in 1992, after crossing the North Atlantic and reaching 80 degrees north in the European Arctic. Bockstoce and BELVEDERE also completed the first eastbound yacht traverse of the Northwest Passage. He was awarded the Cruising Award in 1988, 1991, 1992 and 1993.

J. Gerald Driscoll III and his wife, Dolores, entertain off the California coast aboard ENDYMION. The 48-foot sloop was designed and built by Driscoll Custom Yachts in 1984.

FEAR NOT, a completely restored 16-foot Dyer Glamour Girl is owned by Dudley and Melissa Harrington. Approaching her 45th birthday, she is hull number 14 built by the Anchorage in Warren, Rhode Island.

The New York Yacht Club motto, "Nos Agimur Tumidis Velis," (We are carried forward by swelling sails), as shown on the blazer patch next to the Club blazer buttons, left, was devised at a Club meeting on February 16, 1865, the year the Club was incorporated.

Mr. and Mrs. Martin L. Lyons and friends take their 25-foot Chris-Craft Sportsman SATIN DOLL, built in 1937, for a cruise past the original Elysian Fields clubhouse at Mystic Seaport. The first home of the New York Yacht Club was moved to Mystic in 1949, when SATIN DOLL was 12 years old.

Commodore Donald B. Kipp, below, aboard BLUE DOLPHIN, the motor yacht upon which he lived and cruised extensively, was involved in all aspects of New York Yacht Club life. In addition to serving as Commodore from 1972-1973, he was a trustee for many years, treasurer and a member of the 1970 America's Cup Committee. He owned a series of sailboats named BALLERINA that were a constant presence in fleet activities for many years; the last, his flagship, was a 52-foot auxiliary ketch.

Martin A. "Skip" Purcell, above, takes MIRABELLA into Bar Harbor on the 1993 Annual Cruise.

Commodore Robert G. Stone, Jr., has campaigned his yachts named ARCADIA to a long list of wins; his McCurdy & Rhodes-designed, 69-foot ARCADIA, right, built by Concordia in 1989, is shown here during the Sesquicentennial Regatta. In addition to Class A of the 1990 Bermuda Race, this ARCADIA won the United States Navy Challenge Cup and Royal Yacht Squadron Trophy in 1991, the Edward Welch Clucas Memorial Trophy in 1991 and 1992, and the 1992 Queen's Cup.

Thomas H. Josten, right, is photographed aboard his New York 40, TANIWHA, on the 1992 Annual Cruise; she won the New York 40 Class Astor Cup Day Race Trophy, which she had previously won in 1985, 1986 and 1987. TANIWHA also won the New York 40 Queen's Cup Race Day Trophy in 1979, the Navy Members Cup in 1986, 1991 and 1992, the 1987 United States Navy Challenge Cup and the New York Yacht Club Race Committee Trophy in 1987 and 1991.

ENDEAVOUR, resurrected in 1984 by Elizabeth E. Meyer from its muddy grave in Cowes, England, underwent a five-year restoration process and is one of only two J-boats in commission in the world today. Not only alive but very well, the 130-foot contender for the 1934 America's Cup has added the new sport of "scurfing" to its reticule of diversions; it is shown above broad-reaching at 14-plus knots towing a "scurfer" behind.

Stop Here For Awhile...

The first Library Committee was appointed by Commodore Elbridge T. Gerry on May 20, 1886, and consisted of three members; J. Frederic Tams, A. Case Canfield and A. Cary Smith. Formed to take charge of the books owned by the Club, the Committee was, in addition, authorized to expend in the current year a sum not to exceed $100 to be used for the purchase of books of standard reference on nautical subjects. The library itself was formally established on June 5, 1886. A Finding Index of authors and subjects was maintained until the library moved into the Club House in 1901, when a card catalogue was made available for the first time. The private New York Yacht Club bookplate, placed only in books belonging to the collection, was engraved by Edwin D. French from a preliminary sketch by Walter T. Owens, Esq., in 1900.

By the end of 1913, the library's collection was recatalogued and reclassified following the Library of Congress scheme. The Library Committee report for 1914 states that a librarian was in the Secretary's Office daily and in the library on Monday, Tuesday and Thursday evenings.

The library's collection is a constantly expanding work-in-progress, due in great part from its very beginning to the generosity of members. Today comprising more than 10,000 volumes, it is the world's largest and most prominent private collection of books on ships and the sea, and its historical value is priceless. The chart alcove is an important adjunct of the library, containing over 3,000 world charts in classified drawers.

Most important, the very particular librariness of our library beckons us all to stop for a moment and read. Its look, feel and aroma somehow infuse us with the sensations of the millions of miles at sea and the millions of thoughts about the sea logged by the authors living within its walls.

The locked, climate-controlled Rare Book Room contains many of the Club's most irreplaceable treasures, such as the original minute book, accounts of early voyages, first editions, including the Bowditch American Practical Navigator, and the most complete collection of the Navy Register, from 1800 to the present, known to exist. Librarian Joseph A. Jackson is always eager to share his extensive knowledge of the library and its contents.

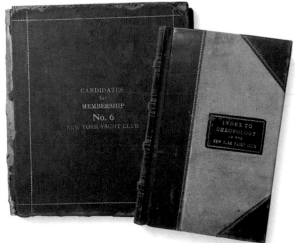

Twenty-five years after INTREPID made its innovative debut, she and her crew members reunited for a weekend of racing and reminiscing. The crew in this 1967 photograph, right, were: in cockpit, from left to right, George D. O'Day, Emil Mosbacher, Jr., Victor A. Romagna. Standing in the background, from left to right: George "Jory" R. Hinman, Jr., Robert A. Connell, Vincent "Bizzy" Monte-Sano, II, Toby Tobin, Ned Hall, Bill Kelly. Seated in foreground, left to right: David K. Elwell, Jr., Samuel K. Wakeman. Above, crew on board for the reunion were: sitting, from left to right, designer Olin J. Stephens, II, David K. Elwell, Jr., Emil Mosbacher, Jr., Samuel K. Wakeman. Standing are, from left to right: Vincent "Bizzy" Monte-Sano, II, George "Jory" R. Hinman, Jr., Robert A. Connell, Toby Tobin, Ned Hall and Bill Kelly.

Briggs S. Cunningham joined the New York Yacht Club on March 22, 1928, which has earned him seniority number one in the 1994 yearbook. A highlight of his extremely successful career afloat was sailing COLUMBIA to victory over the Brittish challenger SCEPTRE in the 1958 America's Cup, the first to be sailed in 12 Metres.

CHASSEUR, Commodore Frank V. Snyder's 50-foot sloop designed by German Frers, won the 1985 United States Navy Challenge Cup and the 1986 Astor Cup.

A. Lee Loomis, Jr.'s 62-foot Sparkman and Stevens–designed NORTHERN LIGHT, right, has been a prominent fixture in Club events since its debut in 1971. NORTHERN LIGHT's long list of wins includes the 1971 Queens Cup, the New York Yacht Club Race Committee Trophy in 1971, 1974 and 1982, the Royal Sydney Yacht Squadron Bowl in 1973, the United States Navy Challenge Cup in 1978, 1979 and 1980 and the 1982 Corsair Cup. For the 1991 and 1992 seasons, NORTHERN LIGHT was co-owned by A. L. Loomis, Jr., and his son A. L. Loomis III. During that two year period, she consecutively won the 1913 Venona Cup, the United States Navy Challenge Cup, the New York Yacht Club Race Committee Trophy and the Cygnet Cup. Thor H. Ramsing successfully campaigned a series of yachts named SOLUTION; his 50-foot sloop, left, designed by K. Aage Nielsen, won the 1964 Una Cup. In 1969, Thor Ramsing presented the Solution Trophy to the Club to be awarded to the boat with the best overall performance in the Annual Regatta.

The Week That Was: The July 1994 New York Yacht Club Sesquicentennial Regatta celebrated the Club's founding with an action-packed week of activities on and off the racecourse that had something for everyone. Intense work aboard the Frers-designed 80-foot LONGHORN, left, sailed by Johan G. Kahm, was typical of the week's racing. Five foreign yacht clubs with whom we share long histories of friendship and competition participated in the event: the Royal Yacht Squadron; the Royal Sydney Yacht Squadron; the Royal Bermuda Yacht Club; the Royal Perth Yacht Club and the Royal Thames Yacht Club.

The July 23, 1994, opening
ceremony of the
Sesquicentennial Regatta,
above, took place at
Harbour Court under blue
skies and the eyes of more
than 2,000 spectators, four
of whom were, below,
Charles, Clark, Carol and
Carter Robertson.

L. Scott Frantz's TICONDEROGA, left, designed by L. Francis Herreshoff in 1936, set the record for the 1940 Miami-Nassau Race. BLACK KNIGHT, above, has served the New York Yacht Club long and handsomely as the Race Committee vessel. Designed by Eldredge-McGinnis, Inc., and built by Goudy & Stevens in 1968, it was an elegant presence at

the very busy Sesqui-centennial Regatta start and finish lines. Visiting flag officers included, left to right, Royal Thames Yacht Club Vice Commodore John O. Prentice, Royal Sydney Yacht Squadron Commodore Norman J. Longworth, Royal Perth Yacht Club Commodore John M. Flower and Royal Yacht Squadron Commodore Maldwin A.C. Drummond.

CONSPIRACY, far left, a Mumm 36 owned by Donald M. Elliman, Jr., David K. Elwell, Jr., George R. Hinman, Jr., and Richard S. Werdiger, was first in class in the 1994 Onion Patch Series and the 1994 Newport to Bermuda Ocean Race. Above, George F. "Fritz" Jewett, Jr., Thomas A. Whidden, Lucy Jewett and Dennis Conner aboard STARS & STRIPES 87 in 1994. James B. Hurlock, Jr.'s Frers-designed 51-foot sloop WHITE-JACKET, left, was built by Nautor and won the 1990 and 1993 U.S. Navy Challenge Cup.

Charles A. Robertson's 12 Metre CANNONBALL was designed by Bruce Farr and Ron Holland and built for the 1987 New Zealand challenge for the America's Cup. CANNONBALL was shipped from Nagoya, Japan, in late 1993. Robertson sailed to sixteen 12 Metre class victories in 1994. The commemorative sesquicentennial pin was sent by the New York Yacht Club as a gift to its members.

Rear Commodore Robert L. James has skippered his New York 40 CARRONADE, right, to many class and other honors, including the New York 40 Class Queens' Cup Race Day Trophy in 1980, 1981, 1985, 1986 and 1988, the New York 40 Class Astor Cup Race Day Trophy in 1988 and 1993, the Royal Sydney Yacht Squadron Bowl in 1988 and the 1988, 1993 and 1994 Navy Members Cup.

Twelve Metre racing was an exciting part of the Sesquicentennial Regatta.

Former Commodores William H. Dyer Jones, Emil Mosbacher, Jr., Robert G. Stone, Jr., and Robert W. McCullough reunited for the closing ceremony, right, that was attended by more than 2,000 members and guests.

163

TICONDEROGA, above, and A. Robert Towbin's 94-foot SUMURUN, left, designed and built by Fife & Sons in 1914, are beautiful reminders that the past is very present. TICONDEROGA set the course record for the Trans-pacific Race in 1965, at an average speed of over 10 knots, and broke that record unofficially in 1969.

The pre-race parade of the New York Yacht Club fleet around Newport Harbor, above, was a fun-for-all procession that gave the thousands of sailors racing in the Sesquicentennial Regatta the opportunity to do a little checking-out of the downtown scene while providing a spectating opportunity for land-side observers.

Five days of the Sesquicentennial Regatta's week of racing and evening festivities honored the five visiting foreign yacht clubs. Celebrating the Royal Yacht Squadron day with Roxanne Leighton, right, are Royal Yacht Squadron Commodore Maldwin A.C. Drummond and Jillie Drummond.

Newport Harbormaster Jake Farrell addresses the audience of 2,000 members and guests at the July 23, 1994, Sesquicentennial Regatta opening ceremony. Behind him, left to right, are Commodore Brian W. Billings, Royal Bermuda Yacht Club, Commodore Maldwin A.C. Drummond, Royal Yacht Squadron, Vice Commodore John O. Prentice, Royal Thames Yacht Club, the Reverend Mary Johnstone, New York Yacht Club Commodore Charles M. Leighton, Thomas E. Hazlehurst, Rhode Island Governor Bruce Sundlun, New York Yacht Club Vice Commodore Alfred L. Loomis III, New York Yacht Club Rear Commodore Robert L. James, Sesquicentennial Committee Chairman Charles A. Robertson and New York Yacht Club Secretary Peter M. Ward.

New York Yacht Club Rear Commodore Robert L. James, right, and Royal Sydney Yacht Squadron Commodore Norman J. Longworth.

George M. "Dooie" Isdale, Jr., shown here with daughter Elizabeth Cochran and son-in-law George Cochran during Sesquicentennial Week.

Roxanne Leighton and Royal Thames Yacht Club Vice Commodore John O. Prentice.

Commodore William H. Dyer Jones, Richard A. Von Doenhoff and A.R.G. Wallace.

Vice Commodore A.L. "Chip" Loomis III and his wife, Elizabeth.

Ulla Hansen and Robert S. Gates.

Race Committee Chairman Andrew A. Scholtz and his wife, Claudia.

New York Yacht Club Commodore Charles M. Leighton receives the CAMBRIA bowl from Royal Thames Yacht Club Vice Commodore John O. Prentice.

Marty Livingston, Angela Fischer, Edwin G. Fischer, M.D., and Stanley Livingston, Jr.

Following the closing ceremony and picnic attended by more than 2,500 members and guests, a display of pyrotechnics ended the July 30, 1994, final evening of the Sesquicentennial Regatta with a bang.

Royal Bermuda Yacht Club Commodore Brian W. Billings and Commodore Robert G. Stone, Jr.

Above, New York Yacht Club Commodore Charles M. Leighton presents the New York Yacht Club Trophy to Royal Perth Yacht Club Commodore John M. Flower and Vice Commodore Kelvin J. Quinlan.

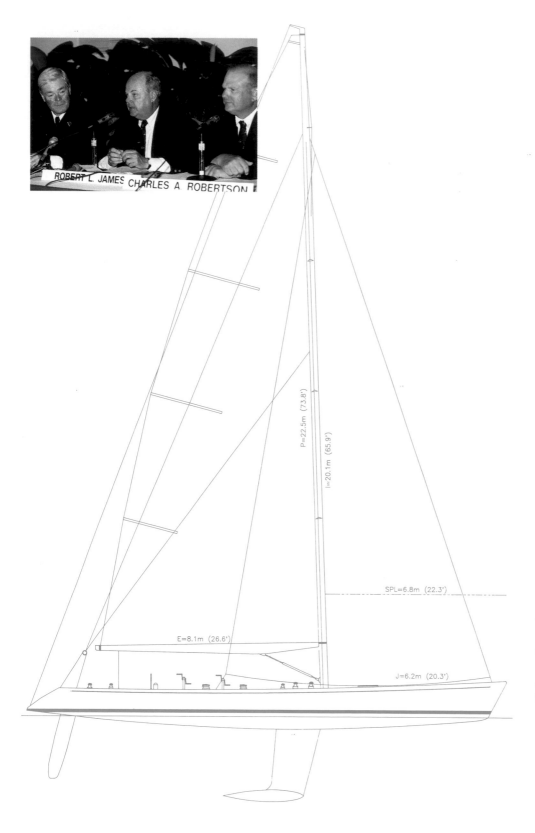

ROBERT L. JAMES CHARLES A. ROBERTSON

On August 28, 1994, the New York Yacht Club International Cup, an amateur match-racing event to be competed for in the fall of 1996, was announced by Commodore Charles M. Leighton, Rear Commodore Robert L. James, Charles A. Robertson and Royal Yacht Squadron Commodore Maldwin A. C. Drummond, left. The event will be sailed in the NY 18 Metre, a new yacht which will be built to a measurement rule based on a design and specifications prepared for the purpose by William Cook. It has been created to provide racing among the world's most renowned and competitive yacht clubs. The event will be conducted by the New York Yacht Club every three years in waters off Newport, Rhode Island, following trial races and an elimination series for both challenging and defending yacht clubs. The format for the International Cup will be the best four of a seven match-race series. The first challenger of record for the International Cup is the Royal Yacht Squadron. Designed by Tiffany & Co., the New York Yacht Club International Cup was conveyed to the Club in a Deed of Gift from Robert L. James and Charles A. Robertson.

Acknowledgements

Writing this book was much more difficult and much more fun than I had imagined. Foremost, I thank my husband, Dudley Harrington, who shared every moment of it, and whose help and support meant everything.

Our great and dear friend Robert H. Clark, Jr., introduced us and this project to Mowry Mann and the Greenwich Publishing Group, for which I am indebted to him. Mowry Mann is one of those people we should all be lucky enough to meet one day; a nice man of consummate style who surrounds himself with talent. This book looks the way it does because Mowry Mann brought Clare Cunningham to its design. Thank you, Clare, for this handsome display of the Club's treasures most of us never knew we had. Tim Connolly, of the Greenwich Publishing Group, has also worked particularly long and hard on this book.

Indeed, there would not be a book without New York Yacht Club Librarian Joseph A. Jackson. Joe's knowledge and expertise about the history of the Club is vast; in addition, he knows where everything is. I thank Joe for the hours he devoted to this book and to me, in addition to his considerable daily duties. When Joe Jackson comes to you with a document in his hand, saying "I don't know if this would be of any interest," you're home free. Thank you, Joe.

I'm particularly happy to thank Geraldine Zelenick; not just for her instant, constant and wise counsel, but because I have a great new friend.

Mrs. Ann Carroll was always a great source of facts on short notice; Stewart L. Gamper contributed his own special knowledge. Plus, he sent me flowers.

Dan and Mimi Dyer are world-class experts on the Bermuda Race, and could not have been more generous with their knowledge, which they unfailingly supplied when I called with no time left. Michael J. Pesare, Associate Director of the Herreshoff Marine Museum, was a particularly precise supplier of facts. Howard Pierce and Mitch Neff at Sparkman & Stephens are resident experts who always responded instantly. I particularly thank Olin Stephens, the greatest master of all, for describing his boyhood sails around Edgartown Harbor and for bringing me up to date on his view of our world.

David P. Tunick, Chairman of the Model Committee, shared his vast knowledge of the model collection at all times of the day; Dyer Jones knows everything about the Club, large and small, where it is, ever was, or is likely to end up. Commodore Robert W. McCullough was there when it all happened, and remembers it as if it were yesterday.

Robert C. Towse, Jr., supplied quickly needed facts without benefit of advance notice regarding the Vineyard Race; Harry Curtis went to great, inconvenient lengths to deliver his scrimshaw to the photographer. Andy Scholtz provided race results almost before the races were over; Jim Gubelmann sent me away staggering with boxes of his family's treasures.

Augie Boehm will be surprised to be mentioned here; I thank him for teaching me enough about bridge to understand Harold Vanderbilt's genius, and to suspect answers I don't know the questions to. I have, however, learned to recognize a finesse when I see one on or off the racecourse.

I heartily thank John Rousmaniere for his time and the precision of his considered thoughts; to be vetted by John is to sleep soundly at night.

Bill Roman, Amy Eisenlohr, Rebecca Edwards, Kirsten Mixter and Carlyn Schroeder of the Edgartown Yacht Club helped greatly to facilitate the flow of information.

This book exists because Charles A. Robertson insisted that I write it. His vision was steadfast, and he was right. Thank you, Charlie.

This book is dedicated with all my heart and love to my wonderful father, Robert W. Hubner. Dad knows more than all of us put together. And not just about boats and sailing, but that, too.

Credits

p. 74   *ENDEAVOUR deck, 1934,* ©Rosenfeld Collection, Mystic Seaport Museum, Inc.

p. 75   above: ©Rosenfeld Collection, Mystic Seaport Museum, Inc., from the collection of the New York Yacht Club Library

p. 76   *Off The Wind, 1937,* ©Rosenfeld Collection, Mystic Seaport Museum, Inc., Image Acquired In Honor Of Franz Schneider.

p. 77   *Burgess and Vanderbilt on RAINBOW,* ©Rosenfeld Collection, Mystic Seaport Museum, Inc.

p. 78   *Mr. Sopwith at the wheel of ENDEAVOR, 1937,* ©Rosenfeld Collection, Mystic Seaport Museum, Inc.

p. 80-81 ©Dan Nerney, 1980

p. 84   ©Rosenfeld Collection, Mystic Seaport Museum, Inc., from the collection of the New York Yacht Club Library

p. 85   photograph by Underhill Studio. (New York Yacht Club Library)

p. 86   *BOLERO crew – Newport-Annapolis Race, 1953,* ©Rosenfeld Collection, Mystic Seaport Museum, Inc.

p. 87   *BOLERO, N.Y.Y.C. 1954,* ©Rosenfeld Collection, Mystic Seaport Museum, Inc.

p. 88   article by Bill Wallace, *New York Herald Tribune,* September 25, 1958

p. 89   *COLUMBIA & SCEPTRE,* John Hopf photographer. (New York Yacht Club Library)

p. 90   *Bus Mosbacher, 1967,* ©Rosenfeld Collection, Mystic Seaport Museum, Inc.

p. 91   ©Rosenfeld Collection, Mystic Seaport Museum, Inc., from the collection of Commodore Emil "Bus" Mosbacher, Jr.

p. 92-93 *GRETEL & WEATHERLY, 1962,* ©Rosenfeld Collection, Mystic Seaport Museum, Inc.

p. 95   below left and right: artifacts courtesy of James B. Gubelmann

p. 96   ©Medalic Art Company, courtesy of James B. Gubelmann

p. 96-97 *CONSTELLATION, 1964,* ©Rosenfeld Collection, Mystic Seaport Museum, Inc.

p. 98   *RANGER, 1937,* ©Rosenfeld Collection, Mystic Seaport Museum, Inc., Image Acquired In Honor Of Franz Schneider

p. 99   George Silk photographer, *LIFE* Magazine ©Time Warner, courtesy of Commodore Emil "Bus" Mosbacher, Jr.

p. 100   *Towing Tank, 1965,* ©Rosenfeld Collection, Mystic Seaport Museum, Inc.

p. 101   above: *INTREPID's deck, 1967,* ©Rosenfeld Collection, Mystic Seaport Museum, Inc.

p. 102   ©Dan Nerney, 1967

p. 103   above: *Intrepid – America's Cup, 1967,* George Silk photographer, *LIFE* Magazine ©Time Warner, courtesy of Commodore Emil "Bus" Mosbacher, Jr.
         below left: *America's Cup Trials, 1967,* George Silk photographer, *LIFE* Magazine ©Time Warner, courtesy of Commodore Emil "Bus" Mosbacher, Jr.

p. 104   ©Dan Nerney, 1970

p. 105   ©Dan Nerney, 1980

p. 106-107 ©Dan Nerney, 1974

p. 107   above right: ©Dan Nerney, 1986

p. 108   above: Arthur Knapp, Jr., photographer. (New York Yacht Club Library)
         below: ©Dan Nerney, 1980

p. 109   ©Dan Nerney, 1977

p. 110   *FINISTERRE,* ©Rosenfeld Collection, Mystic Seaport Museum, Inc.

p. 112   ©Story Litchfield

p. 113   ©Tom Leutwiler, 1988

p. 114-116 ©Dan Nerney, 1980

p. 117   above: ©Dan Nerney, 1980
         below: ©Dan Nerney, 1979

p. 118-119 ©Dan Nerney, 1983

p. 119   right: ©Dan Nerney, 1990

p. 120-121 ©Dan Nerney, 1983

p. 122   above: ©Dan Nerney, 1983

p. 123   ©Dan Nerney, 1983

p. 124-125 ©Dan Nerney, 1989

p. 126   above: ©Onne Van Der Wal, 1994

p. 127   below left: ©Onne Van Der Wal, 1994

p. 128   Arthur Knapp, Jr., photographer, 1962

p. 129   above: ©Dan Nerney, 1982

p. 130-131 ©Dan Nerney, 1970

p. 133   below: ©Natalie Dickinson, 1989

p. 134   ©Tom Leutwiler, 1972

p. 135   below: courtesy of Arthur F. F. Snyder

p. 138   postcard courtesy of Arnold M. Baskin, M.D.

p. 138-140 ©A. Depolo, 1993

p. 141   photograph by Cunningham Brothers

p. 142   left: ©Dan Nerney, 1989
         right: ©Dan Nerney, 1988

p. 143   ©Dan Nerney, 1988

p. 144   above left: courtesy of Harry Curtis
         above right: John J. Rafferty Photography
         below: courtesy of Alexander T. Van Rensselaer

p. 145   above: courtesy of Robert L. James
         below: courtesy of Earl McMillen III

p. 146   ©Bob Grieser

p. 146-147 ©John Bockstoce, 1993

p. 147   above right: courtesy of Melissa H. Harrington
         below right: courtesy of Martin L. Lyons

p. 148   above: ©A. Depolo, 1993
         middle: courtesy of Commodore Donald B. Kipp
         below: Geri Zelenick photographer, courtesy of Commodore Robert G. Stone, Jr.

p. 149   above: courtesy of Elizabeth E. Meyer
         below: courtesy of Thomas H. Josten

p. 150-151 above: ©Dan Nerney, 1985

p. 152   above: J. H. Peterson photographer
         below: courtesy of David K. Elwell, Jr.

p. 153   above: ©Dan Nerney, 1983
         below: courtesy of Commodore Frank V. Snyder

p. 154   *SOLUTION,* ©Rosenfeld Collection, Mystic Seaport Museum, Inc., from the collection of Thor H. Ramsing

p. 155   courtesy of A.L. Loomis III.

p. 156-157 ©Onne Van Der Wal, 1994

p. 158   above: ©Onne Van Der Wal, 1994
         below right: ©Onne Van Der Wal, 1994

p. 159   above: ©Dan Nerney, 1994

p. 160   ©Dan Nerney, 1994

p. 161   above: ©Dan Nerney, 1994
         below: ©Onne Van Der Wal, 1994

p. 162   *"Cannonball" Glides Through Waves Sailing to Windward, Newport, RI,* ©Onne Van Der Wal, 1994

p. 163   above: ©Dan Nerney, 1994
         middle: ©Dan Nerney, 1994

p. 164   above: ©Dan Nerney, 1994
         below: ©Onne Van Der Wal, 1994

p. 165   above: courtesy of Melissa H. Harrington
         below: ©Onne Van Der Wal, 1994

p. 167   below right: photograph by Nancy V. Waggoner

p. 170   ©Onne Van Der Wal, 1994

All other photographs and historical items courtesy of New York Yacht Club Library.

Photography of New York Yacht Club artifacts by Timothy J. Connolly.

Index

Bold listings indicate photograph.